Homeschooling With Purpose

Homeschooling With Purpose

Candid Encouragement for Homeschool Parents

Jenna Lynn Myers

First published by Living With Purpose Press, LLC 2026.

For more information on books and other products by Jenna Lynn Myers, visit thesophisticatedteacher.com

All curriculum and statistics listed herein are accurate at the time of publication but may change in the future or cease to exist. The listing of curriculum and resources does not imply publisher endorsement of all product and company viewpoints.

Editing by Angela Deni

Library of Congress Cataloging-in-Publication Data
Names: Myers, Jenna, author.
Title: Homeschooling With Purpose : candid encouragement for homeschool parents / Jenna Lynn Myers
Description: [Ashburn, Virginia] : [Living With Purpose Press] | 2026
Identifiers: LCCN 2026906532 (print)

First edition ISBN: 979-8-9952744-0-7

A Note from the Author

It took me longer than planned to write this book, as I chickened out for a time. It isn't easy to put yourself out there and to wonder if it will be well received, but I decided it was worth the risk. Why? I care more about encouraging and equipping homeschool parents, than my own discomfort and this book will do just that.

I want this book to be a source of encouragement for homeschool moms, dads, and even grandparents. It was written for those thinking about homeschooling, just starting out, or knee deep in it and in need of hope and encouragement.

I wanted this book to feel raw, honest, and vulnerable, because just the highlights on social media or the unflattering headlines are not a true glimpse into homeschooling.

I hope that it will be a blessing to your homeschool journey.

With love,

Jenna Lynn Myers

A special note of thanks to my husband for always encouraging me and pushing me to do great things. My children, for inspiring me. The many homeschool moms who showed me the way and the ones who stand beside me daily on this journey. My sweet and kind editor. My friends and family who have offered me unwavering support and who continue to lift me up.

Contents

Introduction

A Little About Me

Before we dive in, I feel it is important to introduce myself and to explain a bit of my background. I'm Jenna Lynn Myers, a mother to three growing young men, a wife to a very outdoorsy and kind husband, a dog mom, a cat mom to two sweet rescue kitties, a lover of all animals, a voracious reader, a baker of birthday cakes, a weightlifter, and a fortysomething woman.

But what matters most for you (and this book) is the fact that I am a homeschool mom to three very different learners, a former classroom teacher, and the owner of an award-winning educational consulting and tutoring company. I also hold a master's degree in education. During the course of homeschooling and running my business, The Sophisticated Teacher, I have evaluated and consulted with well over 1,800 homeschoolers and their families. I have been gifted with the opportunity to speak at events to encourage homeschool moms, and I have spent ample time on the board of two homeschool organizations as well as volunteering for a large homeschool nonprofit.

I am passionate about helping families make homeschooling successful and watching their children grow academically. This book has developed from a place of wanting to serve others in the homeschool community, to support them through their journey, and to encourage them with real-life experiences and anecdotes.

My faith has played a role in my motherhood, my teaching, my homeschooling, and now in my business. So I will refer to aspects of my faith throughout this book, because it is something important to me and something that keeps me grounded. While this is not a book about faith, I could not completely leave out something that has impacted so much of my journey.

Why Did I Choose to Homeschool?

To be honest, I am not sure that I chose to homeschool. It practically chose me. I was a classroom teacher in the public school setting for many years, and then I became a technology specialist and part of the admin team for the public school system—yet, here I am, homeschooling. Quite honestly, I think some of my teacher friends were shocked when I left the classroom to homeschool and took it as a slap in the face.

Well, here is my little secret: I am still shocked, too. This was never my master plan. I didn't decide to homeschool long before I had children. Actually, I had decided quite the opposite. I had dreamt of teaching down the hall from where my children sat in class. Their little feet would scurry into my room after school so they could tell me about their day as they bounced joyfully around my classroom. I had a vision for myself, too: homeroom mom coordinating parties and events, chaperoning field trips, and buying end-of-year teacher gifts.

But God slowly laid on my heart the idea of homeschooling. And, boy, do I mean slowly. I didn't fully understand what was happening at the time, but God planted seeds that grew steadily over weeks, months, and years. It started small, as I began to encounter homeschooling families. The first was a sweet, veteran homeschool mom who also ran a cake-baking business. I got to know her through cake-decorating classes that she taught, and we became friends, so I spent a fair amount of time in her home. When I would visit, her children were an absolute delight, and her boys were incredibly close. I knew I wanted my children to be as close as hers were. I knew her boys were intelligent, kind, and independent. I remember thinking to myself, "Is this what homeschooling can do?"

Suddenly, I knew several moms who homeschooled. Some were childhood friends, whom I saw on social media. They were homeschooling children of all ages. I reached out to them and asked questions. I was more curious than anything at the time, but genuine. What they portrayed was nothing like what I had seen on reality television.

Around this time, we were searching for a single-family home with a yard. We saw countless homes and were outbid on many. One day, while we were on our daily family walk, we came across a home in our neighborhood that had just been put on the market. It was one of the smaller models but it had a great yard. It was rundown, yet we could see the potential. When we toured the house, I first went through two small doors near the front of the house, which led to a room with a bright bay window. The light was lovely, and it just felt cozy. In that moment a thought came to my mind, "This could be your school room." I literally laughed aloud. What? A school room? I was planning on going back to work in the traditional setting, and while I had met lovely homeschool moms, I was not yet convinced homeschooling was the path for us. Still, the thought lingered. Of course you don't need a school room to homeschool, but it sure did entice the former classroom teacher in me.

Spoiler alert: We bought the house. Shortly after doing so, I ended up teaching for a homeschool co-op. This experience completely altered my preconceived notion of homeschooling and showed me what homeschooling was really like. Yes, dare I say, I found homeschool families normal and fun. No two families were identical, but they did have a few things in common that stood out to me: family closeness, flexible schedules, unique curriculum choices, and well-spoken children.

So my husband and I decided to try out homeschooling, just for kindergarten. After all, I was teaching at a wonderful co-op and our local schools had moved toward full-day kindergarten, which just wasn't something that excited me for my child. What we said would be one year became two, then three, and now, many years later, we've never looked back.

Chapter 1

Why Homeschool?

Defining your reasons for homeschooling and developing a vision.

Why Homeschool?

Defining your reasons for homeschooling and developing a vision

Why I Homeschool

"Why did you choose to homeschool?" I have been asked this question about a million times. (Okay, maybe I'm exaggerating a smidge, but it certainly feels like a million.) Back to the question: why did I choose to homeschool? If you need a quick recap, I explained how I was led to homeschool in the introduction. The reasons why I began were simple, honestly. I felt God was calling me to do so, and I really didn't want my sweet five-year-old at a desk and on technological devices all day.

Our local school district had done away with many of the play-based centers in kindergarten, and recess was just twenty minutes twice a day. Lunch was at tables, and there was no opportunity to get up and wiggle around. I knew my five-year-old boy needed that time.

I mean, have you met a five-year-old? Not only can they ask approximately one hundred questions per day, according to an academic study, at home they can ask approximately twenty-five questions per hour. It has been proven that the number of those questions drop dramatically at school, where teachers typically ask most of the questions instead. This is because time is focused on high stakes testing and little time is available for freedom of rabbit trails. [1]

Why do kids ask so many questions? They are trying to learn. They aren't trying to annoy us (although it can certainly feel that way sometimes). They are trying to explore the world around them. Children are little sponges, especially in those early elementary years. I knew that I wanted the opportunity to answer every one of those little annoying questions from my own children. (Don't gasp. I'm guessing those questions wear you out, too.)

"Mom, why do dogs wag their tails, but our cats don't?"

"Dad, how do car vents work?"

"Mom, how many chicken nuggets can fit in your tummy?"

"Dad, how does a plane stay in the air?"

"Mom, why don't dinosaurs exist anymore?"

"Mom, why do bees go buzz?"

"Mom, can I have a snack?"

Alright, the last one is not really about learning, but it is probably the question I'm asked most often as a homeschool mom. I digress.

---

[1] "What Children Learn from Questioning," *Educational Leadership* 73, no. 1 (September 1, 2015), ASCD: https://www.ascd.org/el/articles/what-children-learn-from-questioning.

Truly, I wanted my child to ask questions and get out of his seat to explore the world around him. I wanted nature hikes; creek time; field trips to the zoo; opportunities to cook and bake together; and time to strengthen fine-motor skills using Play-Doh, sand, and manipulatives. I wanted my child to experience life around him, question every aspect of it, and learn in the process. I knew he would have this opportunity at home.

I also knew my child needed movement. According to the CDC, children ages three to five need to move throughout the entire day, and children ages six through seventeen need a minimum (that is the keyword here) of sixty minutes of moderate to vigorous physical activity each day.[2] Meanwhile, most schools provide physical education classes twice a week on average (lasting approximately thirty to forty minutes, including time spent walking to and from class, listening to instructions, and taking bathroom breaks) and a daily recess of twenty to forty minutes per day (and that's a generous estimate). Those times barely hit the minimum requirement for movement. Anyone who has been around children, especially boys, knows the reality: they need much more movement than just those sixty minutes. (And, for the record, I do, too.) I knew that homeschooling would give my

---

[2] "Child Activity: An Overview," Physical Activity Basics, U.S. Centers for Disease Control and Prevention, published on December 4, 2025, https://www.cdc.gov/physical-activity-basics/guidelines/children.html#:~:text=a%20child's%20age.-,Children%203%20to%205,activities%20for%20children%20and%20adolescents.

child ample time outdoors, moving around and soaking up vitamin D.

These were certainly enough reasons to begin our homeschool journey, and I saw the proof in the pudding. My first child was so happy and was just absorbing every ounce of information he could soak up.

After year one of homeschooling, we decided to continue. Our why was still the same basic premise: outdoor time, movement opportunities, and opportunities to explore and ask questions. But my husband and I realized our list of reasons to homeschool had grown tremendously after our first year:

- Individualized learning. One-on-one learning meant less overall instructional time and an ability to adapt lessons to meet my child's learning needs.
- Field trip opportunities. You name it, we visited it: zoos, nature centers, children's museums, and more.
- Ample sleep time. I strongly believe in a rhythm that allows for good sleep habits, and I love not dragging a child out of bed each morning. Growth spurt? Great, keep sleeping.
- More time together as a family. This one is funny because clearly you are spending more time together when you are homeschooling, but you don't realize how much until you are in it. If my husband had a random day off or got home early, we could go on an adventure as a family or play games together. Also, my boys had more free time to

play with each other, and this strengthened their sibling bonds.

- Flexibility. Sick? Family in town? Gorgeous day? We can shorten school, pick up again another day, and shift things around. (Disclaimer: always adhere to state laws for hours/days if they are imposed.)

- Incorporating God's word throughout our day. For my family, this time is important to keep us rooted in our faith. It may look different for your family. You may incorporate a motto, song, or a family focus throughout the day.

- Reading a plethora of books together, all day, every day. Reading allows us to gather together, calm our nervous system, and opens the door for relaxed and meaningful conversations throughout our day. It typically compliments our units of study as well.

My why had evolved after just one year of homeschooling, and it has continued to do so throughout the years. As my children have gotten older I have continued to homeschool because I want my boys to have a strong foundation in grammar, Latin, and history, all of which are lacking in the school system where we currently reside. I also want my boys to have opportunities to practice public speaking, critical thinking, and logic. As my boys have outgrown the days of Play-Doh, I knew I wanted them to have the time to dive deeper into their interests, so they could find their best path in life. I also knew I wanted them to be able to exercise their minds and bodies in ways that a traditional school setting just cannot provide. The need for movement doesn't just end at age six. Movement is needed at all ages and stages, as is fresh air. They both act as a reset, even for adults.

Why Others Homeschool

According to the National Home Education Research Institute (which is one of my favorite places to gather facts and statistics about homeschooling), parents choose to homeschool for a wide variety of reasons. The reasons behind homeschooling have historically been for religious purposes, and while 58 percent of surveyed homeschoolers still find this to be a driving force, it is far from the top reason for homeschooling. In a 2019 survey conducted by National Center for Education Statistics, 80 percent cite safety concerns, 72 percent cite dissatisfaction in the quality of academics in the traditional setting, 74 percent desire to focus on time with family, 23 percent have special education concerns, 74 percent want to provide moral instruction, 15 percent of those cited mental or physical health concerns, 54 percent feel a nontraditional approach is right for their child, and the remainder choose to homeschool for a variety of other reasons.[3,4]

---

[3] "Fast Facts: Homeschooling," National Center for Education Statistics, accessed February 28, 2026, https://nces.ed.gov/fastfacts/display.asp?id=91.

[4] Brian D. Ray, "African American Homeschool Parents' Motivations for Homeschooling and Their Black Children's

As an educational consultant and homeschool evaluator and as an active member of my local homeschool community, I've met hundreds of parents and have been blessed with the opportunity to hear their whys for choosing to homeschool. Here are some of the reasons I've heard over the past decade:

- My child was bullied at school and needed a safer environment.
- My husband travels a lot for work, and homeschooling allows for more family time when he is home. Sometimes we get to travel with him, too.
- My husband and I both work shift work, typically opposite shifts, so this allows for more family time and more one-on-one time with our kids.
- My child functions better in small group settings than in large classrooms.
- I don't want my child to use technology for schoolwork until they are older.
- I want to be able to monitor my child's access to technology and books.
- We had a teacher who was causing my child anxiety. (As a former educator, this one really breaks my heart, but it unfortunately happens.)
- Our schools are overcrowded.
- My child was bored in class and was just doing busy work.

Academic Achievement," *Journal of School Choice* 9, no. 1 (2015): 71–96. doi:10.1080/15582159.2015.998966.

- I have a special-needs child. While his teacher was nice, she was just spread too thin, and my child wasn't getting what they needed in a classroom setting.
- We like being outdoors and exploring, so this gives us that time.
- I want my child to have a firm Biblical worldview foundation.
- I love being with my kids and want to soak up as much time as I can.
- I was a teacher and I know too much. I know I can do better at home.
- My child has an immunity issue, and keeping him at home and in small groups is much better for his physical health.
- My child is on the pre-Olympic path for gymnastics, so this gives them the time to practice.
- My child has so many interests outside of the basics, and I want time to nurture that.

I could continue, but it is clear that the reasons a family chooses to homeschool are widespread. Overall, the most common themes are that parents want what is best for their children and they want more time together as a family—two reasons that I fully support.

Knowing Your Why Is Crucial

So, why did I start this book with a chapter about the why behind the decision to homeschool? Because I believe the knowledge will center and motivate you when you are running on empty and are ready to throw in the towel. (And that will happen. We will talk more about that in later chapters.) Knowing your why helps when the naysayers come your way (and they will). It allows you to stay focused and grounds you.

Storytime: I am not a runner. My friends know this very well. But after I gave birth to my third child, I wanted to try something new, so I began training for a 10K. It wasn't going well at first because I didn't have a true reason why. So I took a break and really thought about why I wanted to train for this race. My reasons were that I needed a new challenge and my husband was a runner, so I wanted to at least try it for him. I signed up for a 10K and started training with supportive friends. Some were newbies (and very much not runners either) and others were the full-steam-ahead, running-is-my-life type. It was good to have a variety of positive influences. They helped me remember my why, but I also wrote my why down and put it in a place where I would see it and could be easily reminded of it. Knowing my why kept me going.

This rule applies with homeschooling as well. If I didn't have a why, I'd burn out fast. I'd become disillusioned with what others are doing and why they are homeschooling, thus feeling pressure about my own choices. To avoid this, I write down my why each year before school begins. That may seem too often, but I have found (as I mentioned earlier) that my why changes throughout different seasons. The reasons that influenced me to choose homeschooling in the early years are not the reasons we currently continue to homeschool. Change in life is natural, and changes to the homeschooling journey are inevitable as well. Yearly review of

Knowing my why kept me going.

my why allows me the opportunity to shift and modify my why over time. Over the years I have seen benefits to homeschooling that I could not envision before I began or when my children were little.

Here is the thing about homeschool: my vision isn't the only one that matters. Yes, I am the facilitator of my homeschool and I have to dig deep into my why so that I can keep going. But the whys for my spouse and my kids matter, too.

Now, you may be saying to yourself, "Hold on, Jenna. I am the one doing all the legwork in our homeschool. It is up to me to make all the decisions." And I get that; I do. Honestly, I make the majority of the decisions about homeschooling in our home, but not without the input of my husband and children. This may vary from home to home, depending on spousal homeschool support and involvement and your children's ages, but I strongly believe it is important to include them and hear their visions for homeschool. At the end of this chapter I have provided worksheets and questions to guide you through this process.

Does your vision have to include all aspects of everyone's wants and desires? No, that wouldn't be possible. But incorporating your children's vision into your homeschool will help to provide them intrinsic motivation and give them a why when days are long and they are not feeling the school vibes.

My vision isn't the only one that matters

Having your children write out their own goals also allows for ownership of their education and provides opportunities for discernment and decision-making. For example, your ten-year-old may love playing video games, but one of his goals for the year is to start a business and save up for a powered scooter. He has a choice to make: do I spend two hours playing video games or working toward my goal? This doesn't mean we don't allow for downtime, but a vision and goals can help him prioritize and balance his time and stay focused as well. (Bonus: it also takes some of the pressure off the parents and allows for less nagging.)

Now it's your turn to answer a few questions to narrow down your why. Whether you have homeschooled for one year or ten, this exercise will help you focus and stay the course. I strongly recommend revisiting these questions each year. You can fill them out on the following pages. You are welcome to copy them for your own household, so that you can use them year after year with your children and spouse.

Planning Your Vision

What is my purpose for homeschooling? Be specific.

____

____

____

____

____

What are three things that are important to me educationally?

1. ____

2. ____

3. ____

What do I envision our days to look like? Be specific. For example, do you want to go on adventures daily? Do you want margin to read books and snuggle on the couch?

____

____

____

____

____

Planning Your Vision

What am I looking forward to teaching my children at home?

____

____

____

____

____

____

Questions to consider asking your children or reflecting on yourself.
What are my child's interests?

____

____

____

____

____

____

____

Planning Your Vision

What does my child enjoy doing at home?

____

____

____

____

____

What academic area does my child struggle with?

____

____

____

____

What are my child's strengths?

____

____

____

____

Planning Your Vision

What are (realistic) educational goals for my child?

____
____
____
____
____
____

Other thoughts swirling around in my head:

____
____
____
____
____
____
____
____
____
____
____
____

Now that you have answered these questions, take time to reflect on your answers. Meet with your spouse and your children to share your vision and gain insight on theirs.

Now, write a vision statement below. One that you can refer back to throughout the year when things get tough (because, friend, things will get tough).

Chapter 2

Can You Sustain It?

*Just because you can do everything, does not
mean you should.*

Can You Sustain It?

Just because you can do everything does not mean you should

You might be wondering why I am jumping into the topic of sustaining your homeschool life. It seems a little abrupt, since we are just diving in, but the reality is that homeschooling is a lifestyle. Choosing to homeschool likely means changing and reprioritizing your current schedule. Like any life choice, there are trade-offs. There are some activities (for you, your child, or your family) that you will be able to do while homeschooling that you could not add to your plate if your children attended a traditional school. Or you might find that your bandwidth becomes exhausted while homeschooling, and you need to pause some activities for a season.

How will you know what to keep and what needs to go in your schedule? Some of this will be trial and error, and it will be highly dependent on the ages of your children, the type of curriculum you use, and your community. In this chapter I want to share some of my own experiences, in hopes that you will feel comforted in knowing that life ebbs and flows and no one can keep all the balls in the air all the time.

How It Started

When I began my homeschool journey, I was teaching classes at a local co-op and then my youngest joined the co-op to take several classes. It was manageable and new. We were doing a lot of school at home and then exploring the world around us. He had two little brothers, one preschool age and one a baby. I was tired a lot because there wasn't much sleep, but at least the younger ones took naps, so we could all have quiet time (well, some days). We were in a good rhythm, overall. We had friends, and while my husband traveled, it felt manageable. Granted, I was teaching the early grades of elementary school, which does not take as much time as later grades often need. While teaching reading and beginning math skills requires a tremendous amount of patience, teaching one child and then two the following year felt doable in those early elementary years. I had a good balance overall.

And then, just shy of two years into our homeschool life, COVID happened and the world shut down. We were separated from our newly formed homeschool bubble. At first, I loved the calm feeling of only worrying about my children and how we wanted to homeschool. I truly missed our co-op and the friends we had made there, but otherwise it was kind of refreshing to have zero other commitments than my own family. I added a small pod to our life during this era to help my best friend out, as she was in the medical field and virtual school was not the best option for her children. We had neighbors and close family, and for that season, it worked. There was a good rhythm, and my kids were thriving academically and socially. This is so different than many American families experienced during COVID, but homeschool allowed for a unique and positive experience for my family.

As Time Went On

Once restrictions on social gatherings were lifted, I was more than ready to reenter the world of co-ops and activities in full force. I was feeling extremely antsy. I had pent up energy and was ready to go back out into the world. I am a doer, type-A, overachiever, action-oriented, and social person, so it was time to leave our house and be with people. Maybe you have felt this way, too, after a season of rest or forced rest, such as having a baby, dealing with health issues, or caring for loved ones. You get to a point where you want to jump back in. (Or at least I do—maybe some of you are a little more chill than I am.)

So, what did I do? I joined all the co-ops! Really, I decided to join two academic co-ops, plus a field trip co-op, AND a playgroup co-op. I was ready to dive in headfirst. It was a crazy busy year, and you know what? For that year, I loved it. We were out of the house on a regular basis and I felt accomplished, but I was extremely tired when all was said and done. It was great for that season. It is what I needed and what my kids wanted, but it was ultimately not sustainable long term, especially as I managed the growing academic needs of my children, ran a small business, and just dealt with the curveballs that life tends to throw at you. Does that mean I failed by closing the door on two of those things? No, not at all! It just means they were a temporary fit for my family. Just because something ends does not mean it ended for a bad reason. But I knew I could not continue at my current pace without being stretched too thin.

Can You Keep It Up?

Is it possible to participate in multiple co-ops plus work, exercise, meal plan, host a Bible study, and keep up with housework? Sure, you CAN for a short period of time—but is it sustainable? Absolutely not. Eventually something or someone falls through the cracks. Things you once enjoyed and could accomplish with joy will become boxes to check on a seemingly never-ending to-do list. One day you will realize that you are "doing it all," but it's worth asking: Are you doing it well? Are you just going through the motions? Are you finding joy in your day? I have definitely been here. When you reach a point where you feel you are on the hamster wheel of life and you are getting snappy, have no down time, and are really maxed out, it is time to reevaluate.

Ask: What Is Most Important Right Now?

As a homeschool parent you must decide how to prioritize your schedule. In order to do this, you need to ask yourself: <u>what is most important to you?</u> (And keep in mind that you will need to revisit this question often, as your priorities might change as your children, your homeschool, and your seasons in life change.) Your list of priorities could be compiled of many things that relate to both homeschool and the rest of life, including:

- Co-ops
- Field trips
- Time with friends (yours and your children's)
- Exercise
- Keeping up with your home
- Cooking and baking
- Crafts
- Science projects
- Board games
- Reading aloud
- Book work
- Sports
- Church activities
- Caring for a loved one

As a homeschool parent you must decide how to prioritize your schedule

Big Fish vs. Small Fish

I have a tendency to get carried away with all the things we can do and squeeze in. I often need to reel myself back in, like that little bass my son caught this summer on a chilly beach afternoon. He fished all day, and at first, he could reel in the big fish, but it got harder and harder as he grew weary. Then he caught a smaller fish, and his face shined with delight because his joy wasn't found in the size of the fish—it was in the experience. I must ask myself: Am I aiming for too big of a fish for this time in my life? Would I (and my family) be happier with a smaller fish? In other words, am I trying to do too many things?

Let's revisit the main point of this chapter: not everything that is doable is sustainable. Just as my son couldn't sustain reeling in many big fish over a long window of time, I learned that I couldn't sustain the hamster wheel that I was on. Sure, I was "doing it all" (and I would say I was doing it well), but my actions were not without ripple effects. I was tired and, therefore, less patient with those closest to me. (This is where I need to apologize to my husband and children.) I was frequently distracted, and therefore I had a three-year-old looking for attention in ways that were not ideal. I was always on, and therefore I couldn't wind down at night. I was staying up late to check things off my list, and then I did not sleep well because my brain could not shut down.

So yes, I "did it all," but that doesn't mean other areas of my life didn't suffer. Sometimes you don't even realize what areas are suffering until you step back and take a break or reassess. It's a light bulb moment.

Lesson Learned

I have learned the lesson of doing too much more than once over the years. The first time was when I had a baby, a toddler, and a preschooler. I was teaching classes, tutoring, evaluating homeschoolers, helping at my son's preschool, helping to run a women's ministry at church, and coordinating meals at a local shelter. Not to mention, I had the day-to-day demands of running a household and a husband who was traveling quite a bit. But I just kept going. I would tell myself that I'd slow down the next week and there were only a few more weeks of *whatever the current stressor was,* but I knew, deep down, that I wasn't slowing down as I should have.

Instead, I began a workout program. Not a light program. A ninety-day, every day, one-hour-long-per-day program. I knew I needed an outlet, but I had chosen one that required a lot of physical energy at a time when I had little to give, thanks to a baby not sleeping, breastfeeding, and general toddler insanity. Well, one evening, I squeezed one of these workouts in after a very long day. I was overly tired. I KNEW I shouldn't have done it. I could feel my body telling me to stop, that I was too exhausted. Afterward I showered and walked from my kitchen to my living room, except I didn't make it to the couch. You see there is this one (rather annoying) step down into the living room, and in my tiredness, I missed it completely, rolled my foot, and heard a snap. Yes, I had broken my foot in two places. To avoid surgery (which I truly wanted to avoid due to those three young children I had running around), I was put on foot rest for two solid weeks. I could not put any weight on my foot, and it was my right foot, so I could not drive. My husband had to take several days off work, a lovely friend set up a meal train, others stepped in elsewhere (bless them), and I had to sit.

If you know me at all, you know sitting and doing nothing is pretty much the *worst* form of punishment I could receive. It was, however, in this case the best blessing. This was a lesson to me in sustainability. I couldn't hang on to the hamster wheel any longer. I had to get off. I cut back on a few things and found a better balance. (But, I will tell you that this was not my last hard lesson learned.) My point is this: no one can physically, mentally, or emotionally sustain a heavy plate for long periods of time.

Lesson Learned, yet Again

A couple of years ago, my business won two substantial awards. It was a tremendous honor, and it felt great. I had one of those "my hard work paid off" moments. But then I had to check myself. Yes, years of building my business and relationships felt like it was paying off, but it had also been one of the hardest years of my parenting and homeschooling journey. We had a good homeschool year, test scores came back well, and we did a lot of fun field trips, but I was also incredibly burned out.

I was in a season where I had spread myself too thin. My husband spent a good portion of the year traveling for his job, leaving me to do all the things back home. (This was not at all his fault; it was just the nature of our situation at the time.) I was homeschooling, teaching co-op classes, and continuing to run my business. And then in the fall my grandmother became ill. I needed to support her, make decisions about her care, and be involved in her care. Walking with a loved one through illness and then hospice is not easy, let alone when you are trying to homeschool, raise kids, and keep your business afloat. I "did it all," but was it my best? No. Should I have scaled back earlier and asked for more help? Um, yes. I didn't though. I put on a good face and kept going forward, but guess what it cost me? My peace. I was beyond exhausted, and the more that I felt I couldn't control, the more I took on to fill every waking moment.

It caught up with me though. I was getting short with my kids. My house looked like it had imploded, and I was not taking care of my own health. I was eating whatever I felt like (lots of takeout) and definitely not finding time to exercise. I wasn't sleeping well because when you are spread thin in life and have no downtime, your brain can never relax or shut down. That long to-do list was too much, so it was abandoned. Some friendships suffered, too, because I just wasn't quite myself.

I felt like I couldn't get off the hamster wheel of life and adulting. Then I wanted to quit All. The. Things. Literally. Just walk away from my commitments and anything where I had to be "on." This, clearly, wasn't the answer. But I knew I had to slow down. It was clear I needed to step back from certain responsibilities because it was not the season for me to continue them or take them on.

I will say it again: it was not the season.

I did end up stepping back from a couple roles and activities, and I refocused my priorities. Some things also resolved themselves, as they often do. The people-pleaser in me had an extremely hard time stepping back from some of my responsibilities. A few people who were used to me taking on certain roles were not thrilled about the changes I was making. But I am not here to please the world and everyone in it.

My mom used to say, "If someone believes you are only as good as the last thing you didn't do, then they were only using you for what you did do." That is something that rang true during this particular season. Does this mean you shouldn't volunteer or help people? Not even a little. There will always be people who don't appreciate your time, friendship, talents, or gifts, so you do need to recognize these situations, but you also have to decide why you are taking on activities and commitments. Is it to please others? To impress others? To feel accomplished? To give off a certain appearance? Or is it because you believe it is what you are called to do? Is it because it is the right thing for that season?

You also have to decide why you are taking on activities and commitments.

"No." Is a Complete Sentence

Sometimes you do have to say NO. No to the job offer, no to the volunteer position, no to the extra class, no to the social gathering, no to the field trip, no to the co-op, and most definitely no to perfection and doing it all. And I did. Actually, I said no to my dream job while writing this. (No joke. It was the hardest decision of my life, but I knew it wasn't for this specific season. It was a hard pill to swallow.)

So, what happened when I said no? I felt bad at first. I wondered if I would be seen in a bad light or talked negatively about, but I can't control others' reactions. I knew I could only control what I was currently called to do: homeschool, run my home, pour into my marriage (something homeschool moms can easily forget), continue to run my business (stabilize it and slow expansion), and make room for quiet.

Seasons in Life and Homeschooling

Quiet can be uncomfortable. White space on the calendar can feel both freeing and daunting. Free time, for someone with my personality, is hard to manage. I like checklists, schedules, and plans. So free time can be a challenge for me. I needed to step back, or I couldn't fulfill my current purpose. Not well, not with patience, not with grace. Nope. So, here I am in a new season. A season which will be focused on a few important tasks.

It is okay to let go of expectations and past seasons. This is something I must remind myself consistently. Others' expectations of me are not what matters. For me, seasons of endless hours at a local shelter were put on hold so I could focus on my family. Instead, we found ways to continue to serve together, rather than me serving on my own. We donated resources, and I passed the baton, which also means others have the opportunity to step up. Sometimes helping or serving looks like putting in physical time, other times it involves donations and funding, and sometimes it means spreading the word. None of these outweighs the others—they are all important facets to keep our community thriving—but some ways of serving may be more doable in a particular season of life.

In a similar way, my ability to keep up with my house or host changes as my seasons and priorities change. There are times when I have hosted weekly gatherings and times when I need my home to be quiet and my family's sanctuary. There are many seasons where I have decorated for Christmas like we are living in a Hallmark movie and other seasons where the tree barely gets up. No one way is better than the other. The key is to make decisions based on current priorities and bandwidth.

Your homeschool life will go through seasons

Lean Into Your Current Season

Your homeschool life will go through seasons. When you have littles in tow, you are physically exhausted, sleep deprived, and just trying to keep everyone entertained. As your children grow, mental fatigue can become a bigger issue, as you have constant decisions to make about curriculum, transcripts, and next steps. Some of these years you may do a lot of schooling at home, while in other years you may outsource some subjects. Neither situation is better than the other or makes you a more elite homeschool mom. What makes you an outstanding homeschool parent is giving your best self to your children and using the best resources for your family in each season. Whew. Take that burden off, momma. You don't need to teach every subject every year to be successful. It is okay to have help with the littles, help around the house, and help with school through an online class, a co-op, or a tutor. There is no award for "doing it all" all the time. (We will talk about this later in the book when we address burnout). Take on only what is sustainable, because sustainability is the name of the game here. Homeschooling and parenting: they are a marathon, not a sprint.

Things to Ponder

What does your current season look like? Consider commitments, children's ages, and career

____

____

____

____

What are your top three priorities in this season?
Take a moment to list three priorities that keep coming to mind.

1.______________________________________

2.______________________________________

3.______________________________________

Are there things on your schedule that are weighing you down?
Maybe there are things which no longer bring you (or your children)
joy, can those be reevaluated?

____

____

____

____

Are there things you need to let go of or step back from (even temporarily)?

____

____

____

____

____

Other thoughts swirling around in my head:

____

____

____

____

____

____

____

____

____

____

____

Make a solid effort to be a good steward of your time and current resources and abilities.

Meet with your spouse and your children. Ask them if there is anything that they would like to change in terms of your family's schedule and commitments.

Chapter 3

Social Media vs Reality

Why social media can be a mirage

Social Media vs. Reality

Why social media can be a mirage

As homeschool numbers continue to rise, so does its presence on social media. When I began homeschooling, I only followed friends who homeschooled, but then came COVID and the uptick of homeschoolers. All of a sudden there were homeschool influencers all over my feed, pandering new curriculums, quick fixes, workshops, webinars, and tools destined to make all of your homeschool dreams come true and your homeschool life so much easier.

According to the National Home Education Research Institute, homeschooling is currently growing at a rate of about 10.1 percent. There were more than 3.7 million homeschoolers (roughly about 5 percent or so of the school-aged population) in 2020–2021, and it is estimated there were approximately 5.1 million homeschoolers in 2023–2024.[5] No wonder we are seeing more about homeschooling on social media.

---

[5] "Fast Facts on Homeschooling," Homeschooling: The Research, National Home Education Research Institute, last updated February 27, 2026, https://nheri.org/research-facts-on-homeschooling/.

Seeing Dollar Signs

Not only have social media influencers taken note of the influx of homeschoolers, so have publishers, curriculum vendors, and other educational businesses. The one thing all of these groups have in common: they all want a piece of the financial gains that are to be had, especially because this seems to be a revolutionary time in education.

On one hand, this is great because the resources available to homeschool families are pretty much limitless. I mean, as a homeschool mom I have access to curriculum that is of higher quality than what I had access to when I was a classroom teacher in two of the most prestigious counties in the United States. Academic publishers have realized the untapped market in the homeschool world. Then there are entrepreneurs, many of whom are former teachers and administrators, were homeschooled themselves, or are currently homeschooling their own children. They have all realized there is a particular academic or homeschool niche they want to fill: unit studies not found elsewhere, curriculum to make a busy mom's life easier, or tools to help working parents as they homeschool. In short, people have realized that they can make money off of homeschoolers.

as a homeschool mom I have access to curriculum that is of higher quality than what I had access to when I was a classroom teacher

Part of me gets it. Truly. I mean, I began a business tutoring children who were schooled in a variety of ways. Eventually this led me to evaluating homeschoolers, even though I had never set out to do so. I have always tutored and enjoyed encouraging both children and their parents in their academic journey. Then a few homeschool moms asked if I would evaluate their children. I studied the law tirelessly, became an active volunteer for our state's homeschool association, and spoke with other veteran evaluators. This is where my background in education was particularly helpful. I've now grown a successful business evaluating homeschoolers, but I have continued because it truly brings me such joy to see the academic progress of children. It also brings me joy to encourage their parents (and sometimes grandparents) who are, often, worried that they are not doing enough.

One thing I have decided not to do as a business owner is to have a store pushing products and advertising unless I personally use the curriculum and product. Many have told me this is a bad business move, and from a financial standpoint, it probably is. However, I am not in this world to make a quick buck off a struggling mom. I want to be an encourager, not an influencer. Social media is, in general, all about oneself. It is a show starring you (and your kids, if you put them out there). It may sound harsh, but many influencers are not looking out for the interest of others, but rather for their own personal gain.

So that is why, unfortunately, there are a lot of social media influencers and educational companies who are seeing dollar signs and taking over your social media feed with promises of easier days, harmony in your home, and academic success. While some

In short, people have realized that they can make money off of homeschoolers.

of this is possible, many times the influencers aren't even using the products they are pushing. No joke. Holding up a curriculum for a quick reel and photo op is not the same as seeing it in action. So, if you are following a homeschool influencer (or someone who just began homeschooling) and they are pushing a product, dig deeper to find out if they are truly using the product. You might be surprised at what you find. I have inquired about a curriculum or product that has appeared in my feed, and I have asked questions such as: How long have you used this product? How does it fit into your regular homeschool rhythm? What benefits have your children gained by using this product? I normally get a regurgitated answer or one with very little depth because, the truth is, they don't have the answer. They see marketing as their job and, often, it stops there.

To Follow or Not to Follow

There is a woman whom I follow on social media who shares her outfit finds. I really enjoy her content. She is joyful and seems kind. She is also very honest about the clothes she receives. She probably shares dozens of outfits each week, more during the holiday season, yet she only keeps about one quarter or less of what she receives. She doesn't wear the clothes out or fill her closet with them. She just shares the outfits, how to style them, and the links. She makes a great deal doing so and then gives the clothes to friends and family. I so applaud her for honesty, but it also gives a little glimpse into how social media and marketing work.

I've noticed in the past year or two that there has been a huge uptick in social media influencers who are leaving public and private schools to homeschool. Some are doing so for genuine reasons, while others have realized the content it will provide. Yes, they are capitalizing on their children's education to further their influence and to generate more income. You see, when their children are at home all day instead of at school, they use more products and they have more to do. (But hold on for those details.) This leads to more product placement and advertisements. Those links in their stories for the organizers, markers, waffle makers, and books on the counter? Influencers are getting kickbacks for those links, and with thousands of followers, the return can be quite substantial.

Does this mean these homeschool influencers are wrong? I think it really depends. There are genuine homeschool moms and influencers who are sharing products they use and love, and if they get to turn a profit while doing so, good for them! Truly! But there are plenty of other influencers with a team behind them (that you aren't seeing) who are pushing products and curriculum that they aren't really implementing.

I've witnessed several women follow a similar pathway to join the homeschooling influencer scene. (I have either previously followed these influencers or decided to do a deep dive into their content.) At first, the influencer is bubbly, and she posts some great recipes and workouts. Her children attend private school, and then she pulls them to homeschool. When she does this, she makes a pretty big announcement. She then, typically, holds up a new curriculum and makes sure you know you can comment to receive the link to this life-changing resource.

Then, amazingly (and shortly into her homeschool journey), this new homeschool influencer has written a how-to homeschool guide, complete with the curriculum that was making her homeschool successful. Yes, a step-by-step guide with a daily plan (hour by hour) and links to the curriculum her children have been using for a hot second. She markets it daily: how peaceful the choice was, how easy the curriculum has made her life, and how this guide would be life-changing for anyone thinking about homeschooling. I've seen this play out several times. The influencer was never homeschooled herself. She had no background in education. She'd been homeschooling her own children for less than a few weeks or months, yet she had all the answers. All I can think when I witness this is: "Red flag! Run!"

When I scroll through these influencers' comments, I witness a lot of excitement and also so many desperate homeschool moms commenting things like: "Please send me the link. I'm drowning." "I want to homeschool, but I am scared." "Homeschool has been so hard for us, but this sounds like it'll save our homeschooling." "You make it look so easy! We might try it now!" Typically there are hundreds of comments. Some are looking for encouragement and hope. Others came for a quick fix or a guide to get them started.

Honestly, it makes me a little sick to my stomach because I know this is not what real homeschool life looks like. I understand that their hour-by-hour schedule would only last the first couple of weeks, most likely, and that they have barely implemented this new "life-changing" curriculum. I know it is normal to switch curriculums until you find the best fit for your family. I know that doing homeschool the way some of these influencers portray is a surefire way to bring on burnout, but those commenting don't know these things. They are trusting because this person seems to have all the answers and is extremely well put together.

There was one influencer who I noticed had stopped posting much of this content. She still shared some aspects of homeschooling, but she also made a video explaining how homeschooling was much harder than she had originally thought it would be. I was glad she did this. I don't want to discourage moms from homeschooling, but I believe we need to be honest about the ups and downs of homeschooling. Nothing is perfect: not private schools, not public schools, and no, not homeschooling either. This influencer also revealed she had someone cleaning her house top to bottom each week and a part-time nanny for her younger children, who also went to preschool three mornings a week. So, truly, she was only homeschooling her oldest.

Nothing Is Wrong with Having Help

To be clear: there is nothing wrong with having help. There are tons of moms who have nannies, au pairs, grandparents, tutors, and online or co-op classes to help them on their homeschool journey. If that is what makes homeschooling work for your family and you can swing it, by all means do it! I mean, if I could have a live-

we need to be honest about the ups and downs of homeschooling

-in house manager so I could do school with my kids, cook, and bake, I'd be the happiest person alive. Alas, I do not (but my husband is on dish duty and helps with laundry). But I do think influencers are wrong to let people believe they have this perfectly curated homeschool life with zero help when that is not the case. That is a ridiculous amount of gaslighting. I see it on social media pertaining to homeschool and parenting all day, every day. I'm sure you do, too. Behind almost every influencer with a large following is a team. They either have someone editing and posting (and sometimes curating) content, or they have help with their house, meals, or children. There simply aren't enough hours in the day for them to do all the things they portray. I also want to take a moment to say that it isn't healthy to try to do all these things. We will talk more about that in my chapter on burnout.

Homeschooling looks magical on social media: images of children exploring nature and moms smiling while teaching their children in a perfectly organized school room. There are videos of read-alouds and smiles, projects and crafts galore. Personally, I love art projects, science experiments, and hands-on activities, but we cannot do these things every day. While this can be what homeschool looks like sometimes, the daily reality can be hard. It is so easy to get wrapped up in what we think homeschool should look like, but then we are ready to throw in the towel when things become challenging.

That Perfect Social Media Picture

We can make homeschooling an idol. We forget why we are doing what we are doing and start comparing ourselves to those we see on social media. Next thing you know, you are scrolling social media and are more concerned with someone else's homeschool life than your own.

Yes, I have done this. It kills me to admit it, but this book is about truth and I'm going to share mine. I've had moments in our homeschool journey where I found someone else's homeschool experience more joyful and intriguing than my own. There have been moments when we've been in a slump and then seeing their, seemingly, perfect homeschool posts made me want to give up. I've even had a moment of trying to emulate certain aspects of their idyllic experience, in hopes to reach the desired result: a picture perfect homeschool life.

Yes, I sometimes share some Instagram-worthy shots: books piled high with a warm cup of coffee sitting nearby, the science experiment that went off without a hitch, or the art project we completed as a family. All of these things happen in my homeschool, but do they reflect every moment of our homeschool experience? Absolutely not.

There are times where the read-aloud gets shoved to the side because everyone has ants in their pants and I am running short on patience (like when my husband travels or I've had little sleep). The experiment that I had so perfectly planned for our current unit doesn't always go off without incident, or I may forget an ingredient at the store. The art project was fun, but now I have frustrated children and a messy kitchen because my expectations weren't realistic. It happens. My best advice is to make sure you are choosing activities that your children enjoy, and just as important, that you enjoy as well. If you hate it, then maybe skip it? If science experiments aren't your thing, then turn on a video or join forces with another mom or co-op that embraces the mess and many materials needed for science. If read-alouds are draining the life out of you, choose an audiobook instead.

Just because the mom on the most recent homeschool account you have followed bakes the bread, plays the sport, paints beautifully, or dresses up for history doesn't mean you need to emulate that. Remember that the pictures and videos you see are only a moment of her family's homeschool experience. Their entire day doesn't look like that moment, maybe just a small sliver did.

It's a Lie

The perfection we see when we mindlessly scroll? It's a lie. Social media is very much a farce overall and we just hold it in our hands, hoping it can be true for ourselves. We literally hold it in our hands, as we hold our phones and scroll on social media. All of those idealistic moments, they are fun to share and sometimes they ring true, but that isn't the big picture. It doesn't show the tears when math became challenging, the burnt breakfast, or the mom making her way through mountains of laundry while also diagramming sentences. Social media only shows the highlights. It is like watching a movie preview and then seeing the movie in

My best advice is to make sure you are choosing activities that your children enjoy, and just as important, that you enjoy as well

its entirety and realizing it was kind of underwhelming. The truth: real life is as glamorous as you make it. You can enjoy all moments of homeschooling, both the hard days and those days when you feel great about everyone's attention and progress.

There is a social media account I love. The mom is kind of a hot mess (I mean this in the most endearing way—she is real), and I relate. Like, yes, I can pull it together, but are my ducks in a row every day? No. That isn't how we function here. Anyway, she shares videos of her day (but leaves her children's faces off of her social media, which I fully support), and she doesn't only say, "Hey, look at this sourdough I made while my children practiced their Latin and piano and my oldest researched the Great Depression!" Her kids actually do these things and she makes really good sourdough (I do have sourdough envy, mine is mediocre at best), but she also shares when they need a break. She shares when they get on iPads or Nintendo or watch a show because she needs a moment. She shares when a curriculum isn't working for her child. That is real life. Homeschooling can be so full of joy and wonder, but it is certainly not without its challenges.

My Hope

My hope is that I can be an encourager and not an influencer when you scroll my (somewhat inconsistent) social media. I won't air my children's struggles, as that is not fair to them (they are humans and have a right to their privacy), but I will share mine. I am an open-book type and am far from a perfect homeschool mom. Homeschooling is a lot like parenting; you think you have it down and something changes: a child's needs evolve, a curriculum no longer suits your family, your schedule changes, or a big life change happens. So you adjust. I will continue to evolve as a homeschool mom, which means making mistakes and not having all the answers. It also means the way I homeschool and what you see from me on social media may not always work for your family, and there is nothing wrong with that.

You see, that is the absolute beauty of homeschooling. You can be a Charlotte Mason homeschool family but not be exactly like the Charlotte Mason accounts you follow. You can appreciate the classical homeschool approach but not enjoy all aspects shared on a classical feed. You can take recommendations from me or any other homeschool encourager online but not always agree with every statement we express. Your homeschool should be a reflection of you and your family, no one else.

Final Thoughts

You don't need a social media worthy homeschool room to homeschool well. You don't have to use the prettiest curriculum with watercolor images (even though it's mesmerizing). You can homeschool at the kitchen table, on the sofa, and use black-and-white text. Homeschool is only social media worthy, in my opinion, if it is working for your family. So, stop worrying about what you see when you scroll and worry more about what you see when you look around your home during the day.

Your homeschool should be a reflection of you and your family, no one else.

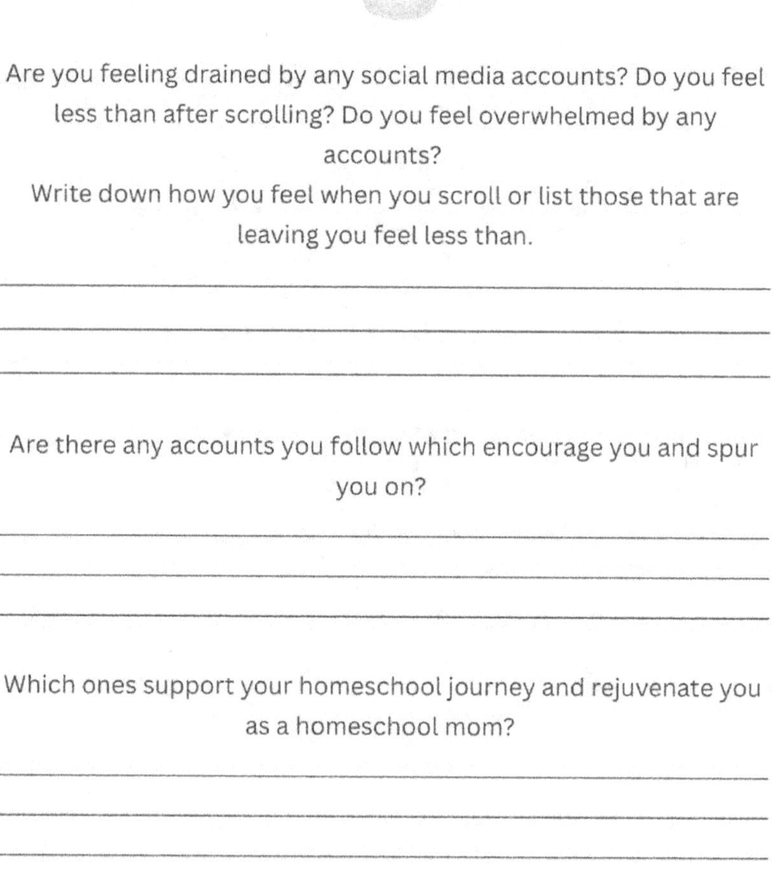

Are you feeling drained by any social media accounts? Do you feel less than after scrolling? Do you feel overwhelmed by any accounts?
Write down how you feel when you scroll or list those that are leaving you feel less than.

____

____

____

Are there any accounts you follow which encourage you and spur you on?

____

____

____

Which ones support your homeschool journey and rejuvenate you as a homeschool mom?

____

____

____

Things to Ponder

When you post on social media, are you doing so for accolades of others? To impress? To just share aspects of your life? Be honest with yourself.

____

____

____

____

Other thoughts swirling around in my head:

____

____

____

____

____

____

____

____

____

____

Take a moment and unfollow accounts which do not
bring joy and benefit to your homeschool.
You can do it. Don't let it make you anxious and
feeling you might miss something. I promise you will
feel relieved once you do it. It doesn't mean they are
awful people, but they aren't the right people for
your social media circle. Yes, social media is big and
wide, but your circle on social media should be
smaller and intentional.

Just as if you were choosing friends to hangout with.

Chapter 4

Permission To Do What You Want

You are homeschooling for your children, not for the approval of others

Permission to Homeschool Your Child, Your Way

You are homeschooling for your children, not for the approval of others

It is so easy to look at what others are doing; measure yourself against their homeschooling methods, curriculum, and schedule; and then feel insufficient as a result. In reality, we all have different methods of teaching, and we are all able to accomplish different levels of homeschool instruction, depending on our homeschool seasons. There is no need to diminish yourself or feel less than in comparison to someone else. You are not homeschooling wrong if your homeschool does not look like the homeschool of the mom next door, the co-op mom whom you look up to, or the random homeschool guru at the park.

Take My Crown

I am the queen of feeling like I am not doing enough in my homeschool. I always wonder what I can do better and if we can add more. While there is something to be said for self-reflection, it is no longer beneficial if it causes me to think I must constantly change to be better or do more. Instead, I have learned that it is okay to be content. It is okay to excel in some areas but not all.

(We are not AI, and we will never achieve perfection.) Fear and doubt tend to creep in when we lose focus.

Fear and doubt may have you questioning: *Can I do this? Am I doing this as well as my neighbor, my friend, or the other moms at co-op? Am I really the best teacher for my children? What if I am failing my children?* These are all questions I have personally faced. There have been times when doubt and fear crept in and I wanted to throw in the towel. It is overwhelming and downright scary sometimes to be in charge of not only your child's physical and mental well-being but also their education as well. Whew. What pressure we can put on ourselves.

Here's the thing: you are the right mom for your child(ren). Yes, YOU, not the seemingly perfect homeschool mom from co-op, the carefree neighbor, or that bubbly mom at soccer practice. You.

We all homeschool in our own individual ways because we were not created to be the same teacher as our neighbor or friend. We each have unique gifts and talents to offer our children.

We homeschool the way we do because we know our children better than anyone else does.

I Thought I Had All the Answers

When I first decided to homeschool, I had two main points of confidence. First of all, I was a classroom teacher (with thirty-six students one year), so clearly I've got this with my own kid. I mean, how difficult could it be to homeschool one kid? Second, it

We all homeschool in our own individual ways because we were not created to be the same teacher as our neighbor or friend.

would be all harmony and rainbows. There would be cuddling and crafts and experiments. There would be bonding and sweetness everywhere. I mean, I love to bake, craft, and read. Easy peasy, right?

There were and still are all those beautiful things, but there were also tantrums, power struggles, impatience, unrealistic expectations, and just life (and, as we know, life can get messy).

Teacher Status

Let's circle back to my first point of confidence: I was a teacher, so I've got this. Guess what? That is partially correct. I had the training and education to teach a wide variety of topics in a large-group setting. Sure, I had worked one-on-one and in small-group settings with students in my classroom, but that is not what I did all day every day. The shift from classroom to homeschool was not easy in some ways. I really had to change my mindset. I was accustomed to teaching from 8 a.m. to 3 p.m. with very few breaks. I mean, how does someone fill those seven hours when you homeschool one kindergartener?

The answer: you don't. At least, you don't fill those hours in the same way that a teacher in a traditional classroom does. I made this mistake, and many first-time homeschoolers (who were and weren't classroom teachers) do as well. *You see, homeschool isn't meant to replicate everything about a typical classroom. Homeschool is about developing a culture of learning while living our everyday life.* It took me quite a bit of time to realize this.

I was so eager about my curriculum choices and all the cute teacher things I chose for our school room at home. I was most definitely replicating parts of my public-school teaching experience at home. This wasn't all bad, but it also wasn't realistic either.

May Appear Different in Mirror

My homeschool routine may very well look completely different from the routine of any one of my homeschool friends. (Yes, even the ones who use the same curriculum and have the same general homeschool philosophy). I'll tell you about my homeschool day, but not until I tell you this: it changes a little each year. It changes because my kids grow older and move to different stages. It changes because our co-op time changes or we add (or remove) an activity from our schedule. It changes because we are human, and while routine is great, keeping the same routine for years isn't always practical.

My Journey

Let me tell you about my first year as a homeschool mom. I taught for a drop-off homeschool co-op all day on Wednesdays. I had a newborn at home and a toddler in preschool a few days a week. So, the first few months were easy, now that I look back on it. (Just like babies feel easy now that my kids are almost teens; every stage has its rose and thorn.) I would drop my preschooler off at his preschool and then come home with the newborn and kindergartener. We would usually play an educational game or work on handwriting and letters or CVC (consonant-vowel-consonant) words. Then I would put the baby down for a morning nap and we would spend one-on-one time for about ninety minutes. (That was way more time than needed for kindergarten, so if you just read that and sucked in your breath, please breathe again. I had the availability, so it worked, but was it necessary? No.)

Plot Twist

About a third of the way through the school year, I pulled my preschooler out of his preschool for his best interests. It was the right move at the time, but it certainly threw a wrench into this perfectly curated schedule. Oh, and that newborn? He was bigger and dropping his morning nap. Now what was I going to do? Shift. Adjust. Be flexible. That's parenthood, and that's teaching, too (even in the traditional classroom setting).

It took a few weeks to get into a new groove with all three of my children. The two older boys took homeschool Ninja Warrior classes and swimming lessons each week, giving us all a little break from each other and a physical outlet during the winter. I still taught at co-op, and my husband (God bless that flexible man) stayed home with the two littles on Wednesdays while I brought my oldest to co-op class.

But, yet again, a plot twist was coming, just a little way down the road: COVID. The pandemic. Lockdown. It was mid-March and our co-op only ran through April, so it wasn't the end of the world, but again we had to readjust just a few months to our homeschool journey. I taught a lovely little pod inside our home, and we did more science experiments than I ever dreamed of. It was an extremely home-based season (as it was for most), but it worked well for my children's ages and our particular situation.

Rhythms Change

As I mentioned in chapter 2, I filled our family's social calendar after lockdowns eased up. Our schedule has changed a little bit each year since then, mostly because my children keep growing older and their needs change. While we continue to do much of our schoolwork at home, over the years my kids have participated in co-ops, social groups, and various classes. Our commitments ebb and flow based on time, interests, and even finances. With upper grades comes a teaching shift for some coursework (someone else is teaching math once we get past pre-algebra), schoolwork takes longer, and my kids' interests are always changing.

When my kids were younger and all in early elementary grades, our days were filled with a little school work, then a break to play or create, outdoor time, reading together, and some more bookwork or hands-on activities sprinkled in. Overall, our schedule allowed for fluidity. It allowed for creative play, outdoor exploration, and just doing life together. Bookwork was a smaller fraction of our time.

As my children have grown, I have found we need more protected time at home to accomplish school work without rushing. For my family, protecting our mornings has been a priority. It allows us ample time to get through our studies and then be able to join classes or friends in the afternoon. With middle and high schoolers, they sometimes need that afternoon time to do work at home, too, or have a study date with friends. But we still work in living life together: cooking, baking, gardening, hiking, and reading aloud even now. The workload has changed, but our priority has stayed the same: doing life together and being intentional in academic and lifestyle choices.

Our schedule and rhythm is just that: ours. Through trial and error we have learned what works and what absolutely does not in our homeschool. We have pivoted with demands of life or with challenges in schooling. My homeschool rhythm works best for my family, but it may not be applicable to yours. This is where discernment, knowing your child, and being intentional in your choices comes in.

Homeschool vs. Traditional School

I am not here to bash traditional schooling. I do have strong opinions on why I believe homeschool is highly beneficial, but I also know that it is not an option for every family for a variety of reasons. I know it is the best option for my family at this time. Could that ever change for us? Absolutely. While I am a huge advocate for homeschooling, I also know life throws you curveballs, and I always want to make decisions about my child's education that will best benefit them as a whole person.

I always want to make decisions about my child's education that will best benefit them as a whole person

For some families homeschooling may be for a season, and for others it's for a lifetime. I am giving you permission—you don't need it, but you may need to hear it—to homeschool as long as it works for you and your children. Perhaps some people may be upset that I am not advocating that everyone should exclusively homeschool, but I believe that is an unrealistic choice for many reasons.

Here are a variety of reasons and seasons why people I know have chosen to homeschool (or not):

- *I have friends who homeschooled during COVID and saw great benefits, but they did not feel called to homeschool long term.*

- *I have clients with special-needs children who tried public school but felt their child was not getting the services they truly needed because the special education teachers were overloaded with students.*

- *I have clients whose children experienced extreme bullying and trauma in a traditional classroom setting, and homeschooling has helped them to heal on multiple levels.*

- *I have acquaintances who were homeschooled, but their parents were rather legalistic and they have zero desire to homeschool because of their unfortunate personal experience. (Don't you hate it when a couple bad apples ruin something? I sure do.)*

- *I have friends and clients who homeschool some of their children while others attend traditional school for sports or other reasons.*

Guess what? Some of my best friends do not homeschool their children. Some of my children's best friends go to private and public school. We can all coexist. You can be strong in your convictions for your family and also realize not everyone is in your same position. (That may ruffle some feathers, I know.) Homeschoolers are protective of homeschooling, as it took such a long time to have the right to homeschool and to show the world how amazing it can truly be. But I won't pretend it is for everyone. That would be a disservice to those committed to homeschooling their children.

A Common Question

Many times, as homeschoolers, we are questioned about our decision to homeschool. It is funny, really. No one says to a child who attends traditional school, "Are you going to do this forever?" I mean, what? When adults ask questions like this, I tend to think, "Are you going to stay at your job forever?" I mean, what kind of question is this? I have no idea what the future holds, so when people ask me if I am going to homeschool, gasp, even for high school, my answer is typically, "If it is what we are called to do and it is working for our family, then yes." Do not allow these questions to consume you or make you question your calling or commitment; rather, let it lead you to a time of reflection in quiet. You do not owe others a five-year plan.

82

You do not owe
others a
five-year plan

Rules, Rules, Rules

When I was a classroom teacher, there were endless restrictions and rules I had to adhere to. Some made perfect sense, while others felt like rules to have rules. Sometimes all I wanted to do was teach in the way I knew my students would thrive. It was such a breath of fresh air when I began homeschooling and could just teach. It took me quite a while to rid myself of some of the rules I once had to adhere to. It felt like I was doing something wrong, but when I let go and saw how my kids were thriving, I knew that it was right to break free from some of the classroom chains I had been trained to stay in.

For example, we love to read aloud as a family, but one of my children is extremely visual, and some books are hard to visualize if you have zero background knowledge. What did I decide to do? I broke the literature rules. We watched a classic movie based on a book prior to reading the book. Gasp! I know. Stop clutching your pearls, though, because my kid lit up later when we were reading the book aloud. He would make comparisons to the movie, and he could play scenes out in his head. It really helped him to focus and retain information. He wasn't confused about separating the two pieces of media. Instead, he was able to see the similarities and differences. It led to conversations about creative liberties and copyright agreements. It opened the door to a whole new level of learning I did not anticipate. Sometimes rules are meant to be broken.

Homeschooling means you are sitting alongside your children as they learn, so you can see in real time what they are comprehending or struggling with. You can adjust as you move forward, and your adjustments do not have to look anything like a traditional classroom or even your friend's homeschool experience. When I supervised student teachers, those who were best stopped to reflect on their students' successes and struggles and then pivoted to meet their students' needs while capitalizing on their strengths.

Reverse Teaching

Reverse teaching or learning is a term a friend and I use often when homeschooling. Sometimes we go to museums, a play, or on a field trip before we dive into material. Why? For the same reason my family watched the movie before reading the book. Because it builds background knowledge. It helps children make connections and strengthens their worldview. Sometimes we will visit a museum, then dive deep into a topic, and then go back to the museum! It sounds like a lot of time, I realize, but field trips are not just fun; they offer tangible learning experiences.

Spending time painting together, listening to music or audiobooks, or exploring nature is time well spent. You are creating a well-rounded individual with a deep understanding of life and all that comes with it. Taking time to teach children how to cook and bake, work on cars, fix something around the house, or garden are all life experiences with ripe opportunities to learn and grow. These experiences can also help children become independent and self-sufficient, which, for my family, is extremely important. These moments also create bonds and core memories for both you and your children. A core memory is one which sticks out in your mind. Taking the time to pass along your skills or learn something new together is a great way to create positive core memories.

Storytime

I am not artistic. I can bake and craft and I would say I am a good cook, but when it comes to the art of painting and drawing, count me out. Stick figures are my go-to, and I am pretty sure if I handed my dog a paintbrush, it would turn out better. But I have a child who wanted to learn artistic techniques. At first, I looked up art classes, which were too pricey at the time and would have been something else added to our plate. So, I decided to learn along with him (and my other children as well). We discovered a quality art program and a brilliant YouTube channel, and off we went. I was utterly amazed (and quite shocked) as I learned many new things alongside my children. And, bonus, we had so much fun doing so. My son ended up giving me some tips. It was such a sweet experience, and we now work it into our school routine throughout the year. I didn't need to be an expert; I just needed to find the right resources and devote quality time to a new hobby where we could all learn.

I have a friend whose son has used an app to learn how to play the guitar. After watching her son learn how to play, my friend started using the app as well. Now she practices just as often (maybe more) than he does. She developed a new talent while homeschooling, and she and her son grew in knowledge together. What a great way to experience life with your child, and what a terrific modeling experience. We are never done learning and experiencing new things. We can pick up a new hobby as a child, a teen, an adult, or, yes, a senior citizen. Maybe the hobby will last only a season, or maybe it'll turn into a lifelong passion or career. What do you have to lose?

It Is an Investment

Homeschooling is an investment. How you invest will depend on your family's circumstances, priorities, and areas of interest. Your investment may look similar to another homeschool family's, but it will never be identical, so do not try to replicate what others are doing. Then your investment would be worth very little, because it wouldn't appropriately apply to your children.

Investing time in your kids and investing in experiences is something you will never regret. (And you don't have to break the bank. There are many free ways to invest in time and experiences with your kids.) No one looks back and says, "I spent too much time with my kids." Nope. Sorry, I have not heard that once. Will all field trips and experiences be sunny, happy moments? No. There will be challenges and frustrations and moments of "Why did I load everyone in the car to hear whining," but there will also be aha moments and joyful outcomes. You don't know until you try it.

Maybe you could choose one new hobby that the family focuses on together or maybe each child could choose something to try (once per week, per month, per quarter—it's up to you). Maybe once a month you plan an outing you wouldn't have

Homeschooling is an investment. How you invest will depend on your family's circumstances, priorities, and areas of interest.

attempted previously. Grab a friend or two if you are unsure. Post in a social media group and ask for tips or others to join if going on your own feels daunting. It doesn't have to cost a lot of money (free opportunities abound) or be an entire day. Start where you and your family are comfortable.

Some of my family's favorite experiences are museums, local nature centers and parks, hikes, exploring nature, and free community events. This may vary depending on where you live, but if you can travel a bit outside your radius and plan out a few future events, I am sure you will find it rewarding, educational, and highly beneficial.

Core Subjects Are Fine, Mostly

While we are talking about throwing out the rules, let's address a question that I hear multiple times each year from clients: *How do I fit in all the subjects? How do I teach everything?*

Let's take away that traditional school perspective that so many of us have engrained. You do not have to teach science every day or every Tuesday and Thursday or even every month. That's right. You can loop, cycle, or unit plan. In the younger years, consistency with reading and math are important. Writing becomes increasingly important as your child develops as well. But in order to spend ample time on these subjects, you cannot always cover other content areas daily or even weekly.

So, I give you permission to mix it up. You could decide the fall is for science and the spring will focus on history and geography.

Maybe you could have four weeks on and four weeks off of particular topics. Or maybe you could devote particular days of the week to different content areas. Maybe you could teach cross-curricular, which means the research paper your child is completing for science counts for language arts, too. You are allowed to double-dip subjects. Homeschool doesn't have to look like each subject is in a separate area on the plate. Mix topics together and hit multiple content areas at once. Just like food can be more tasty when mixed together, magic can happen when you look at a topic from a variety of angles and subjects.

I love teaching in a cross-curricular manner because it allows us to dive deeper into topics and immerse ourselves in the information we are currently studying. We were studying Native Americans recently, and my boys were knee-deep in books, audiobooks, and documentaries. I had another writing activity planned and some general reading comprehension practice to do, but then I took a beat and realized I didn't need to add either of those things because I could easily incorporate language arts into what we were already doing. So we dove deep into local Native American culture, and my children wrote both factual reports and opinion pieces. Based on their studies, my children created a presentation, complete with cornhusk dolls, pottery, and a whittled canoe, and we ended up entering it in a history fair at the local library. It was a rich experience. One that they still talk about. And the knowledge they gained by digging deeper into the content was astounding.

As another example, when my family was studying oceans, I went to a local shop on vacation and bought all kinds of shells. We used them to study bivalves and mollusks. We used a microscope and a magnifying glass to gain more information. We created compare and contrast charts together and then physically categorized the shells. My kids read books about the Prince William Sound oil spill, and we conducted an oil spill experiment. Then they wrote an opinion piece on the topic. They compared types of whales and wrote a research paper. They wrote a persuasive piece on protecting the ocean. We used math when exploring the depth of the ocean and the radius an oil spill impacted. Even shells became a tool to teach basic math concepts. All of this was intertwined throughout a twelve-week study of oceans. My children's writing skills grew, they were reading for a variety of purposes, and they learned how to argue their point of view. It was fruitful in so many content areas. Did we still go over additional math concepts and grammar? Yes, because that is how my brain works. Did I have to compartmentalize each thing? No. I made life easier, but that does not mean educational value was lost. Not even by a long shot.

All that to say: give yourself permission to veer off the curriculum. If working on a schedule and using an open-and-go curriculum is the best way to educate your family, absolutely do it. But I want to give you permission to not check every box of that curriculum. If you skip a lesson or decide to teach in an alternate way, you are not doing it wrong. If the curriculum becomes your Bible, you will probably lose the luster of teaching and lights may grow dim. There is a balance, and it can take a little trial and error to find what is right for your family.

Create and Innovate

When I was a classroom teacher, so many of my students lacked imagination by the time they came to me in fifth grade. Children are meant to explore and create. Homeschooling allows the time for them to be bored and unstructured. This time will lead children to develop new hobbies and interests, start a business, be creative, and stay a kid a bit longer. Boredom and freedom teach children how to solve problems and how to manage their emotions and time.

There are many personal examples I could share when it comes to the fruitfulness of boredom and time. One of my favorites is when my middle son learned about spies and then decided to set up a laser trap in his room. I won't comment on the many bundles of yarn and endless rolls of tape used, but this activity kept him busy for hours. He was problem solving and creating an activity that his brothers later participated in. He was so proud of his creation, and it was so fun to watch his siblings encourage him and take enjoyment in what he created. All three of my children have been given the opportunity to start a small business, and the time at home has allowed them to be creative and thoughtful in doing so. My oldest has been able to further his interest in two instruments and dive into design. Another child has decided ventriloquism is intriguing and spends some of his spare time practicing and watching videos. He is quite comical! It brings such joy to my momma heart, knowing that my kids have the time to seek these experiences. It also helps them find out more about themselves and grows their bond as siblings.

Final Thoughts

Don't isolate yourself or be prideful in your homeschool journey. Share resources with other moms, listen to veteran homeschool moms, and peruse new curriculum, but do not lose sight of why you are homeschooling and who you are homeschooling. The moment you veer from what works for your family to impress others or keep up with others is the moment it will begin to fall apart.

My homeschool bestie is a phenomenal homeschool teacher. She is a history buff and more bookish than I am. Sometimes I envy how she homeschools. I will feel like I am reading a lot of books, but darn it, she always reads more with her children. The truth is, though, her children thrive under her teaching because they are like her and she knows what they enjoy. If I tried to emulate her homeschool methods in my home, we'd be getting on a school bus tomorrow.

Do not let how someone else homeschools their children make you feel bad about how you homeschool yours. Every education has gaps (yes, every single one—traditional or not). There is no perfect scenario, but if you are using your gifts to diligently and consistently teach your children, then homeschooling will be a success.

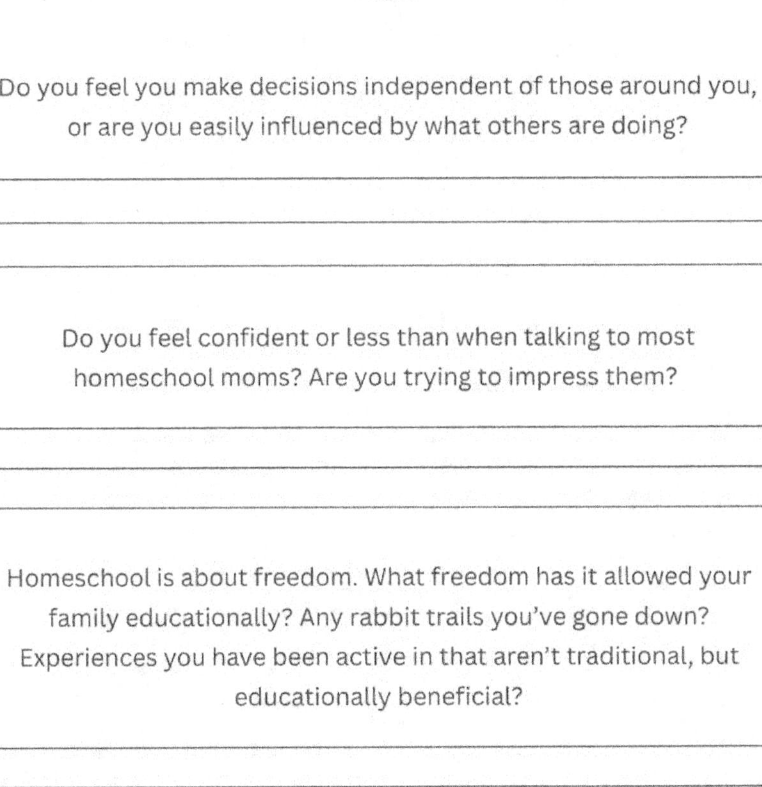

Do you feel you make decisions independent of those around you, or are you easily influenced by what others are doing?

____

____

____

Do you feel confident or less than when talking to most homeschool moms? Are you trying to impress them?

____

____

____

Homeschool is about freedom. What freedom has it allowed your family educationally? Any rabbit trails you've gone down? Experiences you have been active in that aren't traditional, but educationally beneficial?

____

____

____

Things to Ponder

Are you enjoying homeschooling or constantly worried about what else you could be doing and distracted by new and better options? How can you adjust your view if needed.

____

____

____

____

Other thoughts swirling around in my head:

____

____

____

____

____

____

____

____

____

____

Next Steps

Reflect on why you chose your current curriculum, classes, or activities. Are they serving your family or are you doing them to check a box or impress others (or feel good about yourself)? Take time to be honest with yourself and reevaluate decisions as needed.

Chapter 5

The Four C's of Homeschooling

Curriculum, Community, Co-ops, & Cliques

The Four C's of Homeschooling

Curriculum, Community, Co-ops, & Cliques

You may be wondering how curriculum, community, co-ops, and cliques can all fit into one chapter, but you will soon see (or maybe you already have firsthand experience) that they truly do connect.

Curriculum

I cannot tell you how many clients I have met who just want to know what curriculum to use. Which one is magic? Which one will make their homeschool day go smoothly and will make their children geniuses? Which one is the best (and will other parents nod and agree)? Well, I don't have an answer for you because it isn't that simple. Being a homeschooler in today's world means having access to a plethora of curriculum choices and styles. This is both wonderful and overwhelming.

There are a few main categories of curriculum, in general:

- *Charlotte Mason*
- *Classical*
- *Literature-based*
- *Montessori*
- *Open-and-go*
- *Traditional seatwork*

- *Unit studies*
- *Unschooling (which typically doesn't have a standard curriculum)*
- *Waldorf*

Then there is my personal preference: eclectic. My teaching style has never fit into one box. In part this is because I can get bored easily and wouldn't enjoy strictly following a classical, traditional seatwork, or open-and-go curriculum. These styles of curriculum would be too mundane for me, but I do see their value for some children and situations. I love unit studies, but then I want to go down every single rabbit trail, so we can't use units for everything (or we'd never have time to do anything else). Oh, and books! I love literature. Classics, picture books, and everything in between. Does that make me Charlotte Mason or a literature-based homeschooler? Wait, some classical homeschoolers feel this way, too. So, what box do I check when it comes to my style and curriculum choices? Personally, I don't check one.

It is perfectly fine and good to fall into one of the homeschool style categories when choosing a curriculum or homeschool style, but it is also okay to not be married to any one style of homeschooling. I love a classical approach to literature, writing, and grammar. It works for my children, and I appreciate the style. We are unit study people for much of history and science. (We use cycles, but we dive deeper than some classical models.) We use some literature in our unit studies, as many Charlotte Mason homeschoolers do, but I would not call us Charlotte Mason homeschoolers overall (although I do love much of what it has to offer). I simply choose what works for my children's learning styles, abilities, and interests. I also choose the curriculum that I will actually use. The best curriculum is the one you use.

You see, it is possible to buy all the *right* curriculum (which is also somewhat subjective) and still fail miserably. How? If you do not implement the curriculum consistently, it is worthless. Period. Curriculum choices are most certainly important, but consistency is king here. I know a mom who used what some would describe as a more mediocre language arts curriculum. It wasn't super robust and, for some, it may feel lackluster. But this mom was diligent and consistent in her use of the curriculum. No excuses. Her children got the work done religiously and well. And they thrived. They passed standardized tests with ease (well above average) because they retained the information that they were taught and were consistently improving their academic performance.

In contrast, I have a client who bought all the highly recommended curriculum, but it did not bear fruit. Why? Because it was not used as intended or on a consistent basis. This backfired, and I helped the mom make a plan (and find better-suited curriculum) so the family could move forward and make meaningful academic progress. This was not the mom's fault. She was truly doing her best. The curriculum just wasn't the best fit for her or her family. The kids were fighting her on using it, and she was losing the joy of teaching it. It happens to the best of us. (Truly, I have abandoned curriculum before. If it's not working, toss it and find something new!)

The best curriculum is the one you use.

Some curriculum and teaching styles may work for most, but not all, of your children. This is probably one of the more frustrating aspects of homeschooling. It has happened to me! There is a curriculum I absolutely love for teaching reading. I owned it. My first two used it. It's based on the science of reading, and the former teacher in me adored it. So, clearly this was going to work for all of my children, right? Wrong. My last sweet little blondie did not care, not even a little bit, for this curriculum. He whined when we used it and fought me on it. What was his deal? Was it me? Was I tired? Was I not as engaging with him as I had been with the previous two children? Nope. The curriculum just wasn't a good fit for his personality. What a bummer though. I mean, I had already paid for it, and now it is collecting dust.

Oh, and I also had to find a substitute curriculum. He encountered a curriculum that I did not especially care for when I was working part-time at a local private school. The school uses it for early elementary students, and my child, well, he loved it. It uses more of a traditional seatwork approach. (Something I loathe, probably because that is what I experienced as a child and it was most definitely not a good fit for me.) So, what was I going to do? I ordered it. We started with it. He loves it. And he is thriving. (I will admit it is growing on me, but I am also kind of thankful he is the last child I have to teach how to read. Just being honest.) Sometimes we have to bend, be flexible, and take ourselves out of the box we tend to put ourselves (and other homeschoolers) in.

Controversy over Curriculum

Curriculum choices can be quite controversial among homeschool circles. This is where curriculum choice connects to the other three C's: community, co-ops, and cliques. Some homeschool circles and co-ops are extremely picky about their curriculum choices and want to ensure anyone entering their bubble holds the same schooling views. Other communities and co-ops may align themselves with a particular style of homeschooling, but they don't expect everyone to fit the mold to a T.

My Experience

My family was a part of two co-ops when we began homeschooling. One was classical and the other was based more on unit studies and an eclectic mix of subjects. Both served their purposes for our family. Honestly, I truly loved the classical co-op. It used a particular curriculum as its spine, and then some members would add to it (if they chose). Also, while many used the same curriculum at home for math, reading, and history, not all did. And there was no judgment if you chose to use something else. People shared what worked for them, but it was not a constant conversation. I appreciated the wisdom from other veteran homeschool moms, and I also appreciated how every family used whatever curriculum was best for them. The culture and the people were so solid. It was such a positive experience. We are not still with this co-op (sadly) because logistically it no longer works for my family, but our time there helped me be able to identify co-ops and communities that are nourishing.

Our homeschool drop-off co-op was unit-based and eclectic. It was very hands-on and included lots of time outdoors, and it was also a break for me. This was great for a season when my husband was traveling often and I had quite a few family things to attend to. We stayed there for several years, and my children have wonderful memories of hands-on activities and friends they are still close to, but it was eventually time for a change. I no longer needed that reprieve, and my kids were ready to spread their wings.

We are now attending a co-op with our church. For us, this has been extremely beneficial, as our children now see the same individuals at church, co-op, and church-sponsored groups and activities. This has created a very strong community for our family. It is a unit study co-op, which really jives with our family's overall style, and families use a wide variety of curriculum and resources at home. There is a true sense of encouragement and lifting each other up; no one is playing the game of looking down on others' choices or one-upping someone else. The curriculum and community have fit together well for our family.

I do have several clients who have not had favorable experiences when it came to curriculum choice and community. They have felt like a square peg in a round hole—they just didn't fit. Some clients have shared with me that they felt extremely judged for veering from what the majority of their co-op was doing, even though it was the right choice for their child. It led to

do not place yourself or your children (or how they receive instruction) on a pedestal. As soon as you do, it will topple over

awkwardness, hurt, and even being ostracized in some cases. Homeschool parents, I believe that we can do better than this. We should remember that one aim of homeschooling is to do what is best for each child and family. One family is not better than another for using a specific reading, math, or literature program. I offer this warning: do not place yourself or your children (or how they receive instruction) on a pedestal. As soon as you do, it will topple over. Homeschoolers, more than anyone, should embrace others who are making the best academic choice for their children. It is, after all, why many began homeschooling to begin with (and maybe sprinkle in a few other reasons, too). So I urge us all to not become so engulfed in our own preferred homeschooling styles and opinions that we neglect to remember that there is no one perfect way to homeschool for everyone.

Co-Ops and Community

Choosing a co-op that suits you and your family is not always easy, and sometimes it takes some trial and error. (And that's if you even want to attend one; you don't have to!) It can truly take a year or two to decide if something fits or not. First, you must decide what your goals are for seeking co-op and community engagement.

- *Do you want a co-op that takes something off your plate, academically or otherwise?*

- *Do you want to volunteer to teach? Will you be required to teach? To volunteer in another capacity?*

- *Are you attending so that you will meet other moms and families and form deeper connections? Or are you looking to nurture friendships for your children? Or both?*

- *Are you looking for a co-op or community that aligns with certain academic, social, or religious values?*

- *Are you willing to step out of your comfort zone to make this co-op or community work for your family?*

Groups have vibes. Sometimes you walk into a room, and you just know it will work. Other times you have to warm up. And then there are times when you walk into a situation and you feel uneasy. It may not be the group or people themselves, but it is not the right fit for you and your family.

You can create a mini co-op or group if you are not finding what you want or need. I have done this many times over the years. For several years, a few moms and I met in my home to complete a writing curriculum, presentations, and science experiments. It was so much more fun to do in a small community than on our own, and it spread the work out. It wasn't too big where we managed a gaggle of children at every turn, but it also wasn't so small that if one family was sick we couldn't meet up. It was great for those few years, and I loved hosting because I would rather not drive around if at all possible. (And my friends really disliked hosting, so it worked for everyone.) It also allowed the families to form deeper connections and build a solid, encouraging, and uplifting community. Co-ops and groups should support, enhance, and encourage you. If you walk away from a group or co-op feeling drained or unsettled, it might be time to walk away completely.

Let's Get Honest

In all honesty, I have been in that place before. Our family has been blessed with many great opportunities, but sometimes those opportunities run their course and you realize that it is time to move on. It does not necessarily mean that something went wrong, but maybe you or your children outgrow a situation. Or maybe your philosophy on home education changes or you just need a break from adhering to a co-op or class schedule. Sometimes moving on or changing what you are doing is necessary. It can feel hard though. Especially after you pour time, effort, and love into a group or individuals. But change allows for an opportunity of growth, reflection, and new doors to open. It is a part of life.

I know there have been a few moments of my homeschool mom career where I have unintentionally hurt others over an event invite. You cannot always invite everyone to everything, and you may not feel as close to someone as they do to you. (I've been on both sides of this one.) Or maybe you click with the mom, but the kids aren't jiving (or vice versa). I hate to know I have ever hurt another homeschool mom, but I also know it has happened. When I realized I did, I knew I needed to change a few things myself. Chronic oversharer here—if that's a word—who has learned to take time before opening my mouth and sharing details about certain activities, get-togethers, or other times when someone may feel left out.

Cliques and Community

Community is great, but we are human, so cliques happen (whether intentional or not). Sometimes cliques form due to homeschool styles. As discussed earlier in this chapter, some co-ops, groups, and communities only want like-minded individuals. This can lead to cliques, which is something to be cognizant of. I think if we get too legalistic we tend to forget about the freedom of choice in homeschooling. Yes, people naturally gravitate toward people with whom they have things in common. That is expected. But if you pigeonhole yourself in one little bubble, how will you grow?

I hear from clients and I see, often, online how moms want to find their community, but it is hard because homeschoolers are cliquey. I don't disagree. We can be, but there are cliques in public schools and private schools as well, just as there are also cliques in the workplace. But we are not without hope. We can help break the clique by mixing up a group, befriending people with slightly different views or homeschool styles, and then bringing them together. It won't always work, but it can. And you don't know unless you try.

An Example

I run a homeschool moms group for my church, and I was also on leadership for another local homeschool group for several years. These groups have hosted panels of veteran homeschool moms who answer questions from attendees. One year the panel members were quite diverse in their views of education, academics, and continuing education. There were a few intense moments, but they all shared their opinions and experiences honestly and none were bad. They were just different from the person sitting directly next to them. I think it was one of the most fruitful panels our group had ever had! We received copious amounts of positive feedback because their different experiences reached so many people. They opened some moms' eyes and hearts to new avenues of teaching and to what life after homeschooling could look like. (It is not one-size-fits-all). If we had hosted a group of completely like-minded homeschool moms on that panel, it would have been extremely boring and the attendees wouldn't have benefited from the variety of perspectives.

Personally

I love bringing people together. It brings me a lot of joy to help others make connections and to have friends in different circles. Just like I love eclectic curriculum choices and refuse to be locked into one specific homeschooling style, I really can't be put in one box when it comes to community. It doesn't work for my personality. There have been times where I have brought new friends into a situation and it hasn't worked (or behind the scenes others have been annoyed), so that is a risk I run. You can't include everyone, but I do like trying to create opportunities for many to come together. There was one instance when I brought some friends together, and two ended up becoming besties. I am so glad they were able to make that connection. They weren't much alike, but they clicked (in a good way, clearly).

I, personally, do not think it is ever a waste of time to try to make connections with other moms through groups you form, co-ops you join, activities you try, or communities you encounter. You might not keep each of those you meet in your circle for a lifetime—some friendships and connections are only for a season—but you will grow along the way and so will your children. The great thing about homeschooling is that there are a wide variety of opportunities to meet others:

- *Co-op*
- *Church*
- *Sports*
- *Volunteering*
- *Daytime activities*
- *4-H*
- *Clubs*
- *Parks and field trips*
- *Local libraries*

Create Your Own Opportunities for Community

It may seem overwhelming to create your own group or community, but you can do it. A group can have as little as two families or as many as twenty (but maybe not in your home). Here are a few I have created or been a part of in the past (some of which I am still a part of as I type this):

- *Monthly book club (for boys, girls, or both)*

- *Science experiment club (We even met at a pavilion to preserve our homes, and dads joined a few times)*

- *Writing and presentation co-op*

- *Diorama co-op (We made dioramas about any topic and presented them)*

- *Lego and STEM group*

- *Park and playground meet-up*

- *Field trip co-op (We take turns planning weekly field trips)*

- *Play and chat (We drank coffee while the kids played— maybe my easiest and most favorite group)*

- *Unit study group (We studied ecology, geology, marine life, and World Wars)*

You can use a curriculum or choose to play on a mom's (or moms') strengths. You can rotate duties monthly, weekly, or quarterly. Make it something fun and try something that makes you excited.

The grass is always greenest where you water it. So pour in.

You can also create a group for just the moms. Having a monthly gathering for moms can be so refreshing. You can have other moms speak, share resources, share books (fiction or nonfiction), write notes of encouragement for each other, pray for each other, or socialize over tea or margaritas.

Community Is Important

Finding the right community can take time. It is also a two-way street. You cannot just show up to events or a group and sit in a corner. You must engage. You must give so you can get. There are times when you may not be able to give as much, or you need people around you to hold you up and encourage you. To have this, you must also be willing to be that friend and to invest in community. It takes effort, it can be painful sometimes, even awkward, but it is so very worth it. Seasons change, children change, and community changes, but the need is always there. Don't give up. Remember: The grass is always greenest where you water it. So pour in.

Things to Ponder

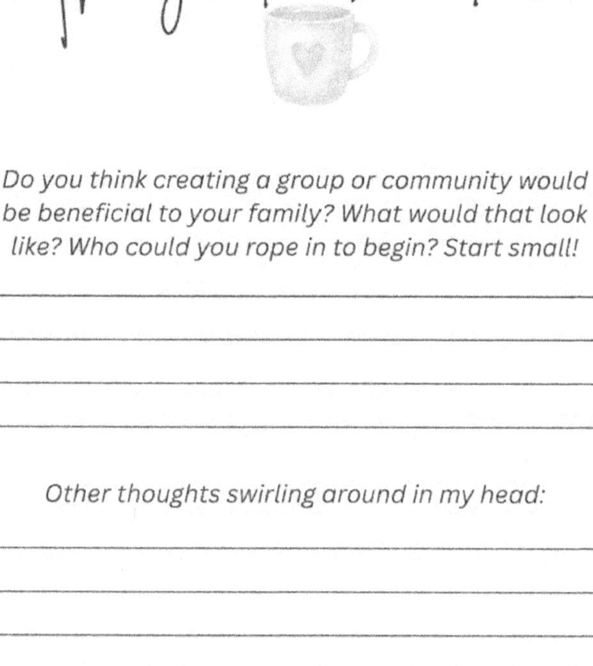

Do you think creating a group or community would be beneficial to your family? What would that look like? Who could you rope in to begin? Start small!

____

____

____

____

Other thoughts swirling around in my head:

____

____

____

____

____

____

____

____

____

____

____

Do you feel you have a homeschool community currently? Why or why not?

____

____

____

Are you spending time trying to impress or fit into a group? How do you feel after your gatherings?

____

____

____

Is it time to walk away from a situation? Or do you need to make more effort and pour in?

____

____

____

Next Steps

Spend some time thinking about another homeschool family (or maybe your general community). Can you pour into that relationship more? Is there a group you have thought about plugging into, but haven't? Now might be the time to go for it. Make it a goal to plan an opportunity for intentional connection with another mom, family, or at your local co-op. Send a text, grab coffee, invite someone over or to the park. You've got this!

If you feel you already do the above things, but it is not reciprocated you may need to evaluate some relationships. Take time to also reflect on your actions: are they not planning or reciprocating because I do not even give them the opportunity? Do I automatically plan and serve but do not ask for help when I need it or input when planning?

Chapter 6

The Age-Old Question of Socialization

Connections are formed everywhere with everyone, not just inside four walls with similar-aged peers

The Age-Old Question of Socialization

Connections are formed everywhere with everyone, not just inside four walls with similar-aged peers

The Number-One Question

The number-one question that I (and practically every homeschooler on the planet) get asked about homeschooling our children: "What about socialization?"

Honestly, this question used to really get under my skin for a few reasons. First, many will ask this question with my children standing in front of them. Rude. Second, many will ask this while my children are literally talking to them, playing, or participating in an activity. (Hi, do you see them in front of you? Yes, they are interacting, and they are doing it quite well, thank you.) Finally, most will ask this question in a snarky way with an I-know-better-than-you attitude, insinuating that if you are homeschooling your children then you are doing them a disservice.

So here I am, addressing the socialization question. I get it on some level. Misconceptions still abound about homeschooling, even though it has evolved a great deal. Not everyone understands that. Some have only heard about homeschooling through one or two very tragic news stories, books, or a reality TV show that highlighted one narrow and extreme situation. You don't know what you don't know. Or, in many cases, you don't believe something could be beneficial and, dare I say, normal until you have experienced it yourself.

I Didn't Fully Understand Homeschooling

Once upon a time, I was a classroom teacher and a very passionate one. I poured my heart and soul into all of "my" children in my classroom, and I knew next to nothing about homeschooling. I thought I knew that it couldn't possibly be better than what I was doing in the classroom. I mean, I was there early and late, I researched and planned, I had several certifications and degrees, and my coworkers were nothing short of amazing. I really could not comprehend why anyone would choose homeschool. So, I will say that I had a generally pessimistic view of homeschooling. (In my defense, my best view of it came from a reality TV show, and that's all I really knew about it at the time.)

Homeschooling is like parenthood and parenting. You don't know what it is like until you experience it. I am sure many of you, like myself, went into motherhood thinking you would parent a certain way and only use particular products and brands. Maybe you stuck to some of those preconceived beliefs, but chances are, once you had your second child, you had no qualms about picking up a pacifier off the floor and quickly wiping it off before popping it back in your baby's mouth. (And, oh yes, I would boil a pacifier before handing it back to my first baby every time one hit the floor. I clearly had too much time on my hands.)

Homeschooling is like parenthood and parenting. You don't know what it is like until you experience it.

Stubbornness, Pride, & Affirmation

I have noticed that many people tend to stubbornly hold to their particular view when it comes to some personal topics, such as education and parenting. (Even veterinary care is a surprisingly controversial topic.) Many people do not want to wrap their brain around a different viewpoint. They feel they have enough information and experience to make up their minds. Period. They have already formed their opinions, and they would have to be willing to let go of those to really hear what another person is saying. Others, sometimes, may feel threatened or personally insulted if they hear you are making a different choice than they are on these sensitive subjects. Most people do not want to have to reflect on their choices. They'd much rather have their choices affirmed and move on.

Have you ever encountered someone like this? They have extreme opinions of the subject of homeschooling and clearly do not want to hear your viewpoint. If you haven't encountered this person, I am going to assume you have magical fairy dust around you or you are smart enough to stay off social media. Be prepared when you defend homeschooling in any form (and especially the socialization aspect) that others may have their own preconceived notions, and they may not be willing to let go of those thoughts no matter what you say.

But guess what: it isn't up to you to convince others that homeschooling is an amazing educational choice. Because truthfully, that is a hard job. When someone questions our decision to homeschool, our instincts tend to kick in, and we want to go all mama bear (or papa bear) on them. We want to give them a laundry list of how homeschooling has evolved, and deep down, you may want your children to shine to prove them wrong. I am here to tell you that you could raise the most wildly successful homeschooled child, and you will still have naysayers. They will call you the outlier. They will still find fault. So, I will say once again:

It is not your job to convince others that homeschooling can be an extremely successful educational choice.

Instead of worrying about what others think, I recommend that you focus on your family and what is right for each of your children. And, yes, the proof will be in the pudding, as my grandmother used to say. For some, that proof will not matter. *But you have nothing to prove.*

Understanding the Socialization Question

When people ask about socialization, they aren't really asking about your schedule or activities. They are wondering how on earth a child could socialize outside of the ingrained, traditional eight-hour school day with same-aged peers. They are really asking if our children can interact with their peers and not be weird. Let's be honest, they are also asking if your child is just sitting at home all day, staring at a wall. Here are a few questions I've gotten from some well-meaning individuals (along with some snarky ones):

"What do they do all day? It isn't like you have a class in your house."
"How will they know how to interact with other kids?"

"Aren't you afraid isolating them will make them weird?"
"But how do they socialize?"
"How will they get a job one day if they don't know how to socialize at a school?"
"Won't they miss out on big things like prom?"
"How will they make friends?"
"How will they make it in the real world?"

There have been plenty of other questions and comments as well, but you get the idea. I am quite certain you've been asked a few of these yourself if you are currently homeschooling, maybe by a neighbor, a friend, a family member, or someone at a store checkout. Again, many of these individuals don't know what they don't know. They have preconceived notions of what homeschooling looks like, and their only experience with daily socialization as a child is the traditional method of schooling.

Former Teacher Here

As a former public school teacher, I can tell you that my homeschooled kids get more socialization than the children whom I taught in a classroom setting. How is that possible? Well, my kids have more time for freedom of play; they participate in activities such as park dates, field trips, and classes; and (in my family's case and many others') they have siblings. Yes, time spent with siblings counts as socialization. I am amazed at how close my children are, and I credit homeschooling for that closeness. Because homeschool (especially in the elementary years) does not take six to eight hours a day, my children have time to meet with friends at the park for two hours, go on a long afternoon hike, take an art class or 3D-printing course in the middle of the day, go ice skating, or just have a friend over. Once we are done with our schoolwork, we socialize. Our social time isn't only a thirty-minute break on a playground or eating a quick (and silent) lunch in the cafeteria, it is typically an extended period of time when my children are forming deeper connections and have the time to play and explore with others.

In contrast, you could put a child in a classroom all day, every day, and they may not socialize at all. They may not have even one friend. I have seen that happen firsthand as a classroom teacher. Perhaps a child is introverted and isn't interested in joining the rest of the group. Or a child may not have much in common with their assigned peers. Just because children are generally the same age and are placed together in a room all day does not mean they will be friends. If you were placed in a room of similar-aged peers all day, every day, you would probably have some conversations, but what if your personalities clashed? What if you had nothing truly in common (other than the fact that you were there learning or doing the same thing)? You might make an acquaintance, and some of us (extroverts and people pleasers in particular) may make a couple friends. But would you be close with everyone? Would it guarantee you a bestie? Absolutely not.

Some will say, "Well, children have to learn to work with and be with all types of people, so they should still experience being in a classroom setting." Can you not have these experiences outside of an eight-hour, five-day-a-week setting? Do sports, clubs, church, co-ops, and other activities not provide similar opportunities? I would argue they do. And, activities outside the classroom typically are with more than only the people in your neighborhood; they are with families outside of your daily bubble.

Personality Accounts for Something

Just like adults, there are going to be children who want to do all the activities and want to socialize daily, and there will be kids who will do one or two activities and then want (need) a break because it's overstimulating and a lot of work for them to be "on." I mean, isn't that just normal for adults as well?

Like many of you, I was blessed with three children who are very different socially. Some children are introverts. They enjoy friends and activities but need ample downtime. Big group events? No, thanks. Crowded park and packed activities? Absolutely not at the top of their to-do list. A small group of friends at a park? Yes, please! Activities and classes with twelve or less kids? Absolutely their jam. This does not mean we can always avoid the aforementioned busier scenarios, but knowing our children well enough (and teaching them to know their own personalities) to recognize where they thrive is key. Sometimes a more introverted child must take one for the team, a.k.a. their more extroverted siblings, and attend a meetup or activity where it is chaotic and there are dozens of children. Is it their favorite thing to do? No, but they still have that exposure because that's life. This is an opportunity to teach and equip our children with the skills to make it through events that aren't their favorite. They also learn to sometimes attend things and participate in things not for themselves but for someone they love. But, overall, how an introverted child chooses to spend their social time and what we, as parents, plan for them looks different than what we plan for children who are extroverted.

You may have an extremely social and chatty child. I have one of the chattiest children on earth. That kid could talk to a slice of bread for an hour. He has so much personality and is somewhat performative, as he loves to make his friends laugh and is a great storyteller. Children with an extroverted and energetic personality typically need regular outlets to physically exert themselves and to socialize. Bigger groups are fine with them. Many times they can be a ringleader or just find plenty of children to chat it up with. They tend to love time at co-op, friend meetups, and field trips, so we can ensure their calendar offers these opportunities on a regular basis.

You may also have that happy-medium kiddo. I, myself, fall into this category. They thoroughly enjoy their friends, co-op, and activities, but they are not always seeking to be the center of attention. They may go with the flow in a crowd, they may sometimes need to skip a social event, and at times they may prefer to hang with just one or two friends.

Homeschooling has allowed all of my children to learn what works best for them. They are learning how to recharge their social battery by identifying what events, people, and activities give them life and which ones drain them. They have also learned how to kindly say no to events and people. They recognize there are times when they don't have a choice and they need to have a good attitude and be a team player, but they also aren't afraid to speak up and say when they need a break or if a situation isn't best for them. No, you cannot cherry-pick your children's friends and social situations all of the time, but what a gift it is to be able to teach them discernment and time management while also allowing them the freedom to identify the people, situations, and experiences that either could help them grow as a person or could be detrimental to their mental health. Honestly, my kids are probably more self-aware and can self-regulate better than many adults who still haven't really reflected on what drains and what energizes them. (It took me well into my adult years to figure this one out myself.)

Age Ranges

I have found it to be so fruitful for my family when we socialize with mixed-age groups. It allows for some kids to become leaders (who may not be otherwise), and it allows for new ideas, creativity, and learning to take place.

One of the things that I loved while teaching in public school was buddy pairing. My older elementary students would have a buddy class a few years younger, and they would read to each other, share presentations, or help with a project. It was such a sweet experience. It was special for the younger students because they felt seen by their older peers. Meanwhile, the older students were able to lead, guide, and encourage younger students, and this boosted their confidence and assisted with building empathy skills.

Homeschooling allows for these mixed-age pairings to happen naturally. It begins with siblings. My older children help my youngest and listen to him read. They also read to him, modeling great reading skills, which helps him feel seen and connected. The youngest can bring out the playful and creative side of the "too cool" older sibling. They have deep conversations about all sorts of topics, and younger children will develop a vocabulary that is so much richer because of these mixed-age experiences.

When we meet up with other families at the park or on a hike, children of all ages come together to create games and play. When we attend a field trip with mixed ages, the older children will ask questions that younger children may not have thought of, and the fearless littles will point out things or speak up when older children may feel nervous. During co-op classes and activities, older children are modeling behavior, public speaking, and work ethic for younger children (and parents are modeling for the oldest children). These mixed-age situations also provide opportunities for those who are old souls and those who are younger at heart (socially or emotionally) to connect with other children based on personality, rather than just age. This is similar to how most real-life workplaces function: mixed ages, mixed personalities, and mixed skill sets.

A Few Ways Homeschoolers Do Socialize

This chapter has been sprinkled with ways homeschoolers socialize, but I want to specifically point out a variety of ways that being social fits into homeschool life. Some opportunities for socialization are just a part of living life. As part of a homeschool family, your children will most likely go to the store with you on a regular basis. Yes, this is an opportunity for socialization. My children always talk to others in the stores, whether it is the lady at Costco with samples on a random Thursday morning or a cashier at a register. They pay for their own items. I will give them my card to check out. They are, of course, typically asked why they aren't in school. They have learned to politely explain homeschooling and will sometimes offer a little glimpse into homeschooling if the individual they are conversing with is kind and well meaning. Yes, this puts my children on the spot, but it is another great opportunity for learning and, well, socializing.

We explored co-ops in a previous chapter, but I want to revisit and reiterate a few things. Co-ops and groups offer great opportunities to use and develop social and emotional skills. Many co-ops are similar to a traditional classroom setting, where students are with similar-aged peers, may sit at tables or desks, and have an adult teacher. These types of co-ops allow homeschoolers who value some aspects of traditional learning to work those skills into their homeschool routine.

Many co-ops and groups allow for project learning, presentations, and time to work together, thus providing plenty of social interaction. When children are younger, playgroups and park dates are common among homeschool families. My family has spent many hours meeting friends at different playgrounds or parks. Not only is it a time for children to run, play, and interact, it's also a time for moms to form deeper connections. Playdates in each other's homes and themed groups are also commonplace during elementary years.

Things shift a bit in middle and high school. Teens will still have opportunities for socializing, but their studies will be coming to the forefront. They may sign up for hybrid classes, twice-a-week co-op classes, and daytime and evening sports teams or classes. Co-op or hybrid classes, again, allow for a more traditional experience and allow for group work to take place. Teens may form study groups or form a group to go to the gym regularly with. My homeschooled children (and many others) attend church youth group twice a week and church social events each month. Teens may end up working part-time or taking some classes at a local college once they enter the later high school years. And yes, they still get together at each other's homes, meet to study at a local coffee shop, and play some pickup ball or go for walks together. Life allows us to be as social as we wish and as much as our bandwidth allows. This is true for adults and for those homeschooling.

The Beauty of Choice

I feel like the beauty of homeschooling is found in the choice to cultivate experiences that are truly going to help your child thrive. This doesn't mean there will never be any challenges. Nor does it mean there will never be a situation where your child's feelings are

the beauty of homeschooling is found in the choice to cultivate experiences that are truly going to help your child thrive

hurt or that they will never have an issue with friends. Of course, issues will arise. Nothing and no one is perfect, and that means homeschool settings will still have moments of frustration. This is just part of life and part of growing up, but you as the parent can choose to put your children in situations that fill their cup, not what would cause them constant anxiety.

Quick Facts

According to the National Home Education Research Institute, "Research facts on homeschooling show that the home-educated are doing well, typically above average, on measures of social, emotional, and psychological development. Research measures include peer interaction, self-concept, leadership skills, family cohesion, participation in community service, and self-esteem."[6] A 2017 compilation study of school choice demonstrated that 87 percent of peer-reviewed studies on social, emotional, and psychological development show that homeschool students perform significantly better statistically than those in a traditional school setting.[7]

---

[6] "Fast Facts on Homeschooling," Homeschooling: The Research, National Home Education Research Institute, last updated February 27, 2026, https://nheri.org/research-facts-on-homeschooling/

[7] Brian D. Ray, "A Systematic Review of the Empirical Research on Selected Aspects of Homeschooling as a School Choice, Journal of School Choice 11, no. 4 (November 27, 2017): 604–621. https://doi.org/10.1080/15582159.2017.1395638

So, They Might Be Weird

Let's circle back to one of those homeschool socialization questions: what if your kids turn out to be weird? I have been on the receiving end of this question a few times, and I have seen it used as a weak argument online more times than I can count. As a seasoned homeschool mom, my answer is this: gosh, I hope they are.

I hope they are outliers because they did not lose themselves to the pressures of society and their peers. I hope they stand out because they look less at devices and screens, instead looking into the eyes of humans while speaking. I hope they are exposed to the world but also have plenty of time to be removed and to focus on their own likes, dislikes, opinions, interests, and hobbies. I hope they become so confident in how wonderfully, uniquely, and perfectly made they are that they go against the grain and aren't bothered when others make different choices, too. I hope they are quirky and kindhearted, unhardened by the constant harshness our world brings them. I hope when they face challenges and uphill battles they will not primarily be surrounded by same-aged, immature minds, but instead have many adults and mixed-age friends nearby so they can gain perspective instead of just peer pressure. I realize that I cannot save my children from their testimony, but I can lessen the burden the outside world places on them to conform, affirm, and agree.

It is better for humans to have a smaller circle of friends, with whom we can be unabashedly ourselves, than a large circle of peers among whom we feel alone in their presence.

Final Thoughts

It is better for humans to have a smaller circle of friends, with whom we can be unabashedly ourselves, than a large circle of peers among whom we feel alone in their presence. This is true for both adults and children. While our children will surely still have moments of loneliness, we can give them the tools and opportunities to find themselves and those who lift them up in life. This is a life skill that is best taught in smaller settings and with the guidance of adults who are truly seeking to help children grow emotionally and socially. It also would behoove us, as parents, to not allow children with brains that are very much still developing to lead the charge of socializing our children. If our children are primarily spending time with peers, and not adults, then where is the modeling? It is up to us parents to nurture and guide our children, so they can become adults who can stand on their own two feet in a variety of social situations.

You see, the definition of *socialization* is just to mix socially with others. That's it. It is, in fact, that simple. So, if you need a short answer when asked "how do your children socialize," your answer can be as simple as this: we have plenty of opportunities to mix with others socially.

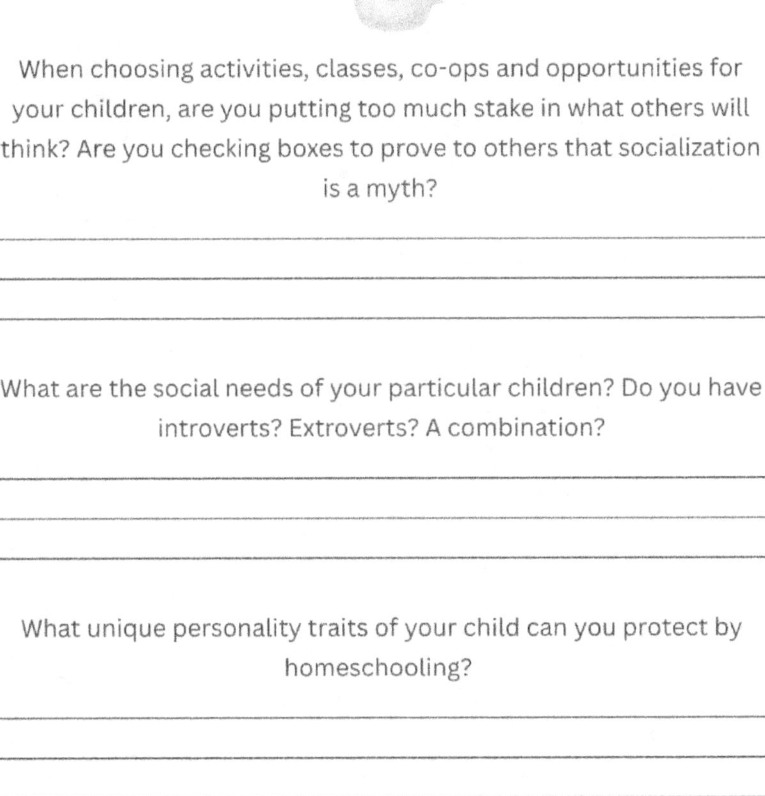

When choosing activities, classes, co-ops and opportunities for your children, are you putting too much stake in what others will think? Are you checking boxes to prove to others that socialization is a myth?

____

____

____

What are the social needs of your particular children? Do you have introverts? Extroverts? A combination?

____

____

____

What unique personality traits of your child can you protect by homeschooling?

____

____

____

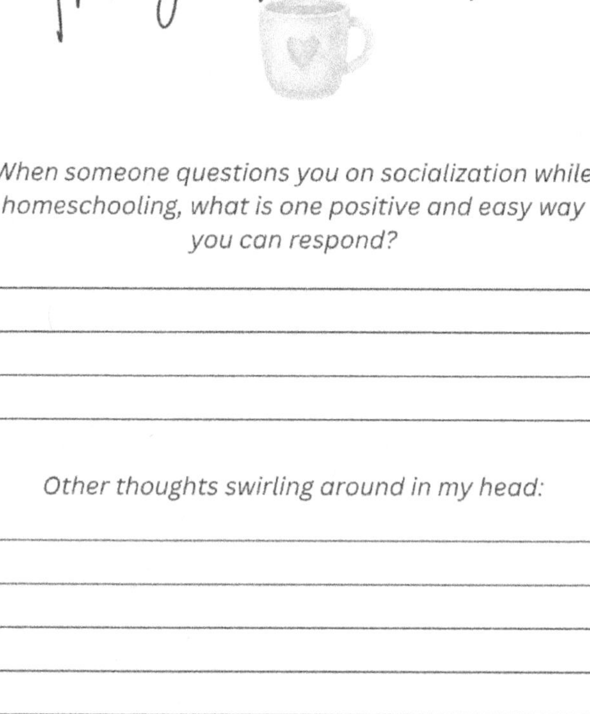

Things to Ponder

When someone questions you on socialization while homeschooling, what is one positive and easy way you can respond?

____

____

____

____

Other thoughts swirling around in my head:

____

____

____

____

____

____

____

____

____

____

____

Next Steps

Developing appropriate social skills is important for all humans, but do not caught up in proving this to others. The moment you do, you will lose sight of why you are homeschooling and you will make decisions which might appease others, but also may not be in the best interest of your children.

Take time to reflect on your schedule and your why, before making social committments. Ensure the social committments you have made align with your reasoning for homeschooing.

Chapter 7

Time have changed, and so has homeschooling.

Dispelling Common Myths about Homeschooling

Times have changed, and so has homeschooling

I have already discussed a few homeschooling myths throughout this book—for example, homeschoolers lack proper socialization or parents need to have a teaching degree to effectively homeschool—but I know there are still a few more myths floating around social media, your brain, and even the news. So, let's take a look at these myths and set the record straight.

Myth: Homeschoolers Are Homesteaders

It is extremely common to hear that homeschoolers are homesteaders who tend to be fairly crunchy. While this certainly can be the case (and I have some quite phenomenal homeschooling friends who do indeed raise sheep, make their own bread, and live on a large farm), homesteading is actually not the norm in homeschooling. While I do bake bread (because it is just so delicious), I also still frequent my local chain grocery store. Many homeschoolers are health conscious and cook their own meals, but the majority of us also love margarita night and some Chick-Fil-A on the way home from a field trip. My family does not raise animals, although we do seem to keep collecting dogs and cats. We live on a quaint cul-de-sac, not a large farm. I have a plethora of clients who live in townhomes, condos, and apartments. Many have zero pets, let alone farm animals, and most do not mill their own grain (I'd like to try it one day though). In short, you do not have to be crunchy, have a farm, or live outside the urban or suburban lifestyle to homeschool.

Personally, homeschooling in the suburbs has been a huge blessing for my family. We have friends in our neighborhood who homeschool, which allows us to have recess in the middle of the day and I have other moms nearby who I can lean on. We are able to quickly get to activities and classes because we live in an area that is easily accessible. We are also able to take walks and ride bikes on paths in the middle of the day. I can host friends at a moment's notice and make a quick run to the grocery store for missing science experiment ingredients. For us, it works.

I have several homeschooling clients who live in the city. They visit museums regularly, walk to lunch when they are tired of doing dishes, and meet up with other homeschoolers at the park on a regular basis. Do not let your location hold you back from homeschooling.

Myth: Homeschoolers Must Have Money

I have most definitely been told that I am lucky I am able to homeschool. I've also had individuals comment that it "must be nice to have the money to homeschool." Can homeschooling be pricey? Yes, it can be. Does it have to be? No. You do not have to be rich to homeschool. You can use your local library, free online programs, and even resources such as YouTube and podcasts to make homeschooling affordable and successful. You do not have to spend hundreds of dollars on classes, co-ops, or curriculum each year. If there is one thing I have learned, it is that the homeschool community is great at selling used curriculum. Utilizing your local social media groups, homeschool conventions, and book sales are also great ways to save money. There is absolutely nothing wrong with purchasing a used curriculum. Remember: just because it is new, doesn't mean it is better.

You can join or start a co-op that has minimal costs. For example, a co-op that my family attends is parent-led, which means that moms (and some dads) take turns teaching. Because we all put in the time to teach, we keep our costs to less than one hundred dollars per year, per child. Also, if you do have extra funds to spend on homeschooling, I recommend being cautious about how you spend them. Just because something costs a lot doesn't mean it is better. My kids have taken a couple of pricier homeschool classes over the years, and I will tell you that I was less than impressed on more than one occasion. There are always companies trying to capitalize on homeschooling, so it is important to distinguish between solid learning opportunities and ones that are costly but don't provide much benefit.

Most homeschoolers are not rich. We are not privileged, minus the fact that we do reside in a country where it is legal to homeschool. Personally, my family has made sacrifices to homeschool, especially early in our homeschool journey. For example, my husband kept his truck for almost twenty years. We didn't (and still don't) eat out often, and we don't frivolously buy items that we do not need. We saved money before we began homeschooling, and my husband took positions where he could earn extra income. From my experiences actively engaging in a homeschool community and running a business that caters to homeschoolers, most homeschool families are in similar financial circumstances. Homeschooling is a lifestyle choice; while it is not always an easy one, it is worthwhile in the end.

Myth: Homeschooling Is for Stay-At-Home Moms Only

"You are just a stay-at-home mom. Must be nice!" It is a little comical when I hear people say this. Yes, I do stay home and homeschool my children. I also work. I run a business. I meet with clients. I tutor. I am a working homeschool mom, as are many homeschool moms I encounter. Here are a few of the careers that my friends and clients currently work while also homeschooling their children:

- *Hair stylist*
- *Marketing and social media specialists*
- *Teacher (both online and in a traditional setting)*
- *Nurse*
- *EMT*
- *Physical therapist*
- *Political analyst*
- *Baker*
- *Piano teacher*

- *Church ministry associate*
- *Therapist*
- *Scientist*
- *Engineer*
- *Nurse practitioner*
- *Dog trainer*
- *Business manager*
- *Federal government employee*

This is just a small sampling. Many I know run their own small businesses, watch other children, or work full-time and, wait for it, their husbands' homeschool their children, too. Yep, dads are capable. I've seen many grandparents step in as well.

Here is the thing: *whether or not you have a career outside of raising your children is not a badge of honor.* There are many dual income homeschool families. I am one of dozens of moms in my own community, who do have a full or part-time job outside of homeschooling. But if you are able to stay home and focus on homeschooling and nurturing your children full-time, then you are working full-time. Period. End of story. Hard stop on this argument. Homeschooling and raising children is a full-time job. That is why other careers (such as teaching and childcare) exist. It takes time, focus, and a boatload of energy to stay home with one's kids, let alone to homeschool. The truth is all homeschool families work hard to make homeschooling work.

Homeschooling is a lifestyle

Myth: Homeschoolers Are Always Large Families

This is a pretty old-school assumption, but some people still think you must have a large family if you homeschool. I know a few, but the majority of the families I homeschool with or hire me as an evaluator have three or less children. I wouldn't call three children large, more like average. You do not need to have six children to homeschool. I actually could not have six children and homeschool, as I am entirely too neurotic for that level of chaos. I do, however, have friends who have large families and homeschool very well. They are tag team parents, with a high tolerance for noise, and just way more laid back than I. It works for them, and that is great, but large families are not a homeschool requirement.

Myth: Type A Personality Needed

While we are on the topic of being neurotic (or, more specifically, the fact that I can be a bit neurotic), let's address how not all homeschool families have Type A moms. Some homeschooling families do have moms who love a good list, need a solid schedule, and clean their kitchens after every meal (which is about 200 times a day when you homeschool), but not all homeschool moms fit this label. I have one friend in particular who is not even Type B, she is more of a Type C (if that is a thing). Kid melting down? That is fine. She'll stop everything without batting an eye, sit right there, and listen. Toddler drew on the wall. Oh well, it gives us character, and that's what Magic Eraser was made for. (Not me. I would be scrubbing the walls immediately!) I am so thankful for these moms who are slightly less neurotic than I. They ground me. They remind me everything is not the end of the world. They have helped me lessen my anxiety and stress over the years. I have also rubbed off on them. I hold them accountable and ensure we are on time for field trips. I create the sign-ups, and they may show up late but always with good snacks and a story to tell. You do not need to fit in one personality box to homeschool. Just find the moms who help bring you balance.

Myth: A Dedicated School Room Is a Must

Alright, I see this myth on social media all of the time, and I am guilty of sharing my school room, too. The perfect school room. It is a room set aside in your home, dedicated only to homeschooling. The colors are neutral. There are bins on the shelves. Books and tactiles are organized so fashionably. The floor is clean and free of Cheerios. While these school rooms look beautiful and are oh-so tempting, they are also not realistic for most families. Yes, my family does have a school room, but it is only clean once a quarter, if that. There are books and paper piles, and manipulatives and games are strewn about. We also don't keep our schoolwork exclusively in this space. Our books and bodies travel all over the house while going about our school day.

You can be just as productive with the corner of a bookshelf in your living room and doing school on the couch or at the kitchen counter. I have clients who are extremely low on space, so they use a bin to store their school books under a bed, coffee table, or couch when not in use. (I think this is a genius idea.) The point you do not need a school room that is beautiful and color-coordinated to have a successful homeschool experience

is this: you do not need a school room that is beautiful and color-coordinated to have a successful homeschool experience.

Myth: All Homeschoolers Are Religious

This is a big myth. Many assume that a family must be extremely conservative or religious if they homeschool. While this certainly can be the case, it is not always true. I would surmise that about two-thirds of my clients do *not* homeschool for religious reasons and do *not* fall into the strongly religious category. There are many religious co-ops and groups for homeschoolers in my area, but there are also a large number of secular groups and classes as well. Homeschooling is not one-size-fits-all. Homeschool families come from diverse backgrounds, cultures, and beliefs. I would caution anyone not to make assumptions about another's political views or religion just because they have chosen a nontraditional educational path for their children.

Myth: Homeschoolers Aren't Prepared for College and the Real World

I addressed this a little bit in the chapter on socialization, but this myth deserves another mention. This old-school myth suggests that homeschooling can academically disadvantage a student or prevent them from getting into, succeeding at, or assimilating in college. This could not be further from the truth. According to the National Home Education Research Institute, homeschool students score 15 to 25 percent higher on standardized tests than their traditionally educated peers.[8] Homeschooling also offers ample opportunity for independent and hybrid studies, as well as the development of strong time management and executive functioning skills, thus making homeschool students much more marketable to colleges and future employers. Most universities view homeschoolers as self-motivated individuals who have already proven their ability to work independently. I have witnessed clients and friends send their homeschooled children to Ivy League schools, the Naval Academy, and top trade schools. Those students have stayed the course and become quite successful. Homeschooling can prepare children for college, life inside and outside the home, and trade school. The key is that parents should be diligent and purposeful in leading their child down a chosen life path and prepared to support that plan with quality curriculum and opportunities, which can include travel, classes, co-ops, internships, and life experiences.

A little note: college readiness is great; life readiness is better. I believe if homeschoolers focus too much on academics and invest too little time on hobbies, interests, exploration, and life skills, then homeschooling becomes no different than a traditional school setting. Don't lose the home part of homeschooling.

---

[8] "Fast Facts on Homeschooling," Homeschooling: The Research, National Home Education Research Institute, last updated February 27, 2026, https://nheri.org/research-facts-on-homeschooling/.

college readiness is great; life readiness is better

Myth: Your Kids Can't Play Sports

This is a huge myth in the homeschool world. While state laws vary concerning participation in public school sports for homeschoolers, talented athletes have many opportunities available to them. First of all, homeschooling can actually allow an athlete more time to practice, giving them a leg up. I wish I had been homeschooled in high school, when I spent every waking hour after school and on the weekend at the barn perfecting my riding skills. Had I been homeschooled, I could have completed my studies in half the time and doubled my practice time. Also, as homeschooling has become more mainstream, there are a growing number of teams and sports organizations for homeschoolers to join. There are a slew of famous athletes in an array of sports who were homeschooled, including Serena and Venus Williams, Simone Biles, Tim Tebow, Blake Griffin, Michelle Wie, Missy Franklin, Bethany Hamilton, LaMelo Ball, and Joey Logano. If there is a will, there is a way.

Myth: A Good Homeschool Day Equals Every Box Checked

Wouldn't it be lovely to wake up, enjoy a hot cup of coffee, check off everything on your homeschool to-do list, and end the day with a clean house and dinner on the table? Surely, that must be how life looks at successful homeschool moms' homes. Nope, this is a myth. It is a lie. One that I am quite certain, most of you have already figured out is a fantasy. If the house is perfect, all the schoolwork is done, mom has showered and worked out, and a home-cooked meal is on the table, mom must have been helped in some way or another. For us, the sign of a good homeschool day is the mess it leaves behind: The science experiment on the kitchen counter. The stack of books on the living room floor. The art project drying in the dining room. A mess means you were so engrossed in your children—living life with them, teaching them, being hands-on—that you couldn't get to every little thing. Maybe you didn't check off every aspect of a lesson today, but your child showed great interest in the science topic, so you watched a video, extended the experiment, or read another book. In other words, you dove in. You went where the passion was and, guess what, they learned something. (It just might not have been something on your checklist.) If you had the time to answer questions, slow down, and practice skills, then it was a productive school day. Checking every box does not mean progress or retention, and it surely doesn't equate success.

Myth: Homeschooling Will Ruin My Relationship with My Child

Homeschooling can certainly have its peaks and valleys, but so does parenthood. From what I can tell, homeschooling will only ruin your relationship with your child if you don't actually educate them (which they will grow up to resent you for) or if you are a drill sergeant. Thankfully, there is a very happy medium on that continuum in which homeschooling can be a place for family relationships to thrive. Teaching is not just about imparting new information; it's about modeling, guiding, and learning alongside your child. Showing our kids that we do not actually know everything and we are also still learning and growing is a powerful way to teach them that we are human. It allows them to see your vulnerability and humility. This allows for trust to continue to deepen. The thousands of hours I have spent with my kids has strengthened our bonds. Yes, sometimes we all need a break from each other, but truly living life together, day in and day out, has given us such a gift. The conversations we are able to have on a daily basis and the depths to which I know my children have strengthened our relationships in ways that I could not have imagined.

Homeschooling isn't about being your child's best friend, but it also is not about control. It is about walking alongside our kids and then loosening the reins but providing an atmosphere where it is safe to ask questions, push boundaries, and become independent. I won't lie, there have been moments where I would like to be just mom and not teacher, because teaching is a huge responsibility and it does add another layer of complexity to my relationship with my kids at times. But homeschooling is also so fruitful. I love that I can drop everything and have a heart-to-heart with my child in the middle of the day. I love that I get to witness and celebrate when reading clicks and math facts stick. I loved the cuddles on the couch when we read books aloud together when they were little. I love the banter back and forth as we discuss novels and current events now that they are older. These are the moments that continue to strengthen our love and respect for each other. Is it easy? Heck, no. Is it worth it? Absolutely.

Final Thoughts

This chapter has addressed just a few of the homeschooling myths that circle social media and headlines. But that is all they are: myths or outdated assumptions. I wish the benefits of homeschooling were far more well-known than the myths. I have experienced so many unexpected blessings while I have homeschooled. The time with family. The strong family bonds. The ability to travel off-season. The deeply formed relationships we have developed. The sense of community. The ability to dive into my children's interests. The time to guide them through life's ups and downs. The way it has made me parent intentionally and thoughtfully. How it has humbled me and made me grow as a mother and as a human being. I am so thankful the myths about homeschooling didn't hold our family back from experiencing it. I wrote this book because I wanted to set the record straight on homeschooling, to share how it has positively enhanced my own family (and countless others' families), and to encourage you to take (and stick with) the opportunity.

It isn't up to you to change the narrative about homeschooling, but please know the narrative isn't always accurate.

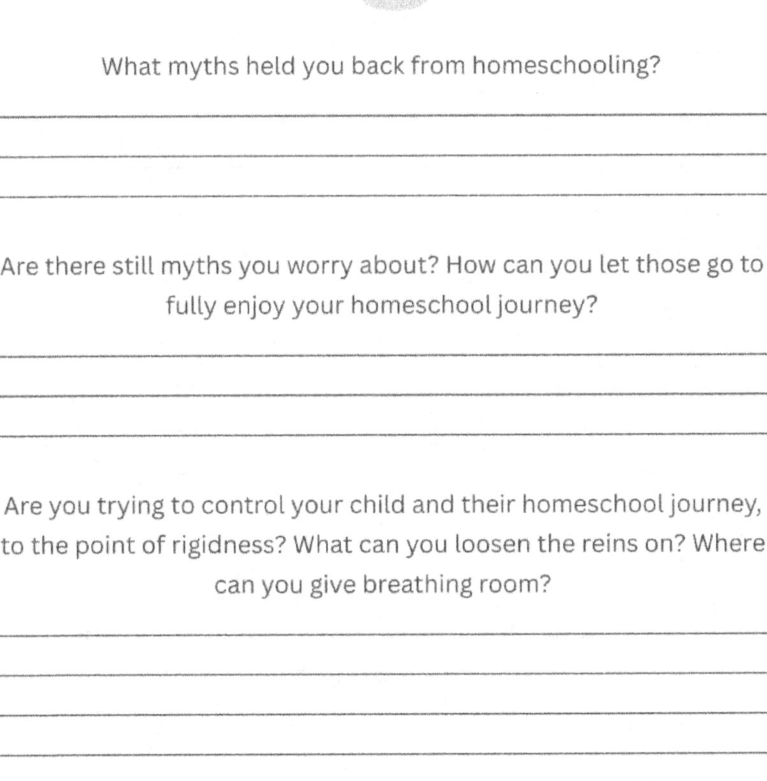

Things to Ponder

What myths held you back from homeschooling?

Are there still myths you worry about? How can you let those go to fully enjoy your homeschool journey?

Are you trying to control your child and their homeschool journey, to the point of rigidness? What can you loosen the reins on? Where can you give breathing room?

How has homeschooling positively impacted your family?

____

____

____

____

____

____

____

____

Other thoughts swirling around in my head:

____

____

____

____

____

____

____

Next Steps

Spend some time reflecting on whether or not you are trying too hard to control aspects of your homeschool because you are worried about dispelling myths for those around you. Remember the journey isn't about proving that homeschooling works for others, it is about making the right academic, social, and emotional choices for your child (and your family).

Now that you have reflected, it is time to have a family meeting, where you can make a list of all the ways homeschooling has benefited your family. Positive reflection will strengthen everyone's desire to continue homeschooling.

We love homeschooling because:

____

____

____

____

____

____

____

____

____

____

____

Chapter 8

Homeschooling a Child with Special Needs

Progress is not always linear, nor does it equate perfection. We should consider progress as moving forward in meaningful ways academically, socially, and emotionally

Homeschooling a Child with Special Needs

Progress is not always linear, nor does it equate to perfection. We should consider progress as moving forward in meaningful ways academically, socially, and emotionally

For some families, homeschooling can look like having children who pick up a book on their own and happily read for hours on end. Some children may fly through a curriculum, and their parent is truly just a facilitator. But for other families, homeschooling can look a little less idyllic, especially those who are homeschooling children with unique needs and learning challenges, whether those challenges are physical, behavioral, or cognitive. For these families, it is not always possible to schedule an hour of reading time each day or choose an open-and-go curriculum with ease. For these families, homeschooling can sometimes feel cumbersome and heavy. For these families, the extra field trips and activities can throw their child off-schedule and create anxiety and frustration in their homeschool life. This chapter is for these families with unique learners.

When You Know You Have a Child with Unique Learning Needs

A significant portion of my clients homeschool children who would fall under special education in a traditional school setting for either cognitive, physical, or emotional reasons. Many were pulled from a traditional classroom because their needs were not met and progress was at a standstill (and, in some cases, even sliding backward). Maybe this resonates with some of my readers. Your child was tested and received an IEP (Individualized Educational Plan). At first school went well—perhaps your child had a rockstar teacher—but then it became clear that the traditional school setting was no longer beneficial to your child. Or maybe, and quite unfortunately, you did not receive the services or support your child needed from the start.

For many of these families, having formal testing results and knowing your child's learning experience in a traditional classroom could be considered an advantage. (However, that would not be the case if the child experienced trauma in the classroom.) Parents will have insight into what was and was not working in the traditional classroom, and test results can give a detailed picture of a child's learning capabilities (as defined by the test). There is a caveat: even in-depth testing does not paint a full picture of any child. It is not holistic. It does not account for diet, sleep, personality (typically), likes and dislikes, or triggers.

This is where the parents are the experts. You have seen firsthand when a group becomes large and your child shuts down

even in-depth testing does not paint a full picture of any child

or gets overwhelmed as a result. Testing may suggest that a particular ability of your child will cap at a level not equal to their peers, but you know that if you tie learning to your child's current interest or obsession, they can be stretched at least a little bit further. Maybe a child's strength will not be writing a five-paragraph essay, but their ability to absorb information through auditory processing and then draw, create, or verbally express their knowledge is extremely strong. If you choose to homeschool after participating in a traditional classroom setting and after completing testing, you will be able to couple the knowledge gained from those experiences with your parental expertise to best pare down curriculum, adapt to your child's learning style, and tailor material to your child's interests and strengths. I am not saying it will be easy, but you will have a whole toolbox of knowledge. What a blessing that can be! Remember, whether your child is neurotypical or atypical, there will be trial and error in finding the best way to reach and teach them. You actually will have a leg up if you can play off of your child's previous educational experiences.

I do want to note that some students need time to decompress, if they are removed from a traditional classroom setting that was harming their physical or mental health. In the homeschool world we call this "deschooling." Allowing your child time to reset their mind and body before diving into curriculum. This does not mean video games and free time all day. It can look like quality time together reading or listening to books, field trips, cooking and baking, interest led learning, and sometimes therapy (mental, physical, speech, to name a few).

When You Start Homeschooling from Day One

Children are complex learners, and it may not always be easy to determine if your child has unique learning needs. However, if you are noticing a pattern of one step forward and two steps backward, an inability to effectively communicate or comprehend, a struggle with writing and dexterity, a consistent frustration while learning to read, or a lack of recall, then you may have a child with unique learning needs. (Please note this is only a brief list of possible identifiers.) If you have a solid relationship with your pediatrician or family doctor (and they are supportive of homeschooling), it can be wise to consider consulting them for initial diagnosis assistance. They can refer you to a specialist, begin basic questionnaires, and help you get the ball rolling. They are not, however, able to thoroughly diagnose. There isn't a one-size-fits-all diagnosis, but formal testing can help narrow things down for your child.

If you are homeschooling and suspect your child has a learning challenge, you can seek testing through your local public school in most states. This is the most cost-effective way to approach full-battery testing. There are many private practices that offer testing, but it is important to ask for referrals from other homeschool parents in your community and to ensure a testing center is homeschool friendly, as unfortunately some are not. The cost can vary, from several hundred to several thousand dollars. If you suspect your child may have dyslexia, dyscalculia, or dysgraphia, then there may be special educators, reading specialists, and speech therapists in your area who could assist with diagnostic testing. Educational consultants, like myself, also often conduct diagnostic testing.

If you have an education background, you may not feel testing is necessary in some circumstances. If you do not, I do encourage you to seek a professional, with a solid reputation and training, to perform at least an observation and review of work samples. This could provide initial insight and help determine whether or not you need to move forward with diagnostic testing and to what extent. Testing uses standardized educational and psychological measures of behavior. It is one piece of assessing a child's abilities. Typically, you use testing in conjunction with anecdotal notes and evaluation.

Testing can be beneficial for a few reasons:

- *It is objective, which either solidifies your concerns or relieves you of them if your child is working at an appropriate level for their age.*

- *It gives you more information about how your child's brain works. What a gift it is to know more about your child.*

- *It can help you understand what teaching methods and curriculum would best benefit your child.*

- *It can drive your schedule and goals.*

- *It provides information so you can more fully understand your child's strengths and weaknesses.*

- *It allows your child to have accommodations when completing standardized testing (including SATs and ACTs)*

- *It can help differentiate between behavioral issues versus learning disabilities, allowing for appropriate support and pivoting, as sometimes the two can mimic each other.*

- *It can give you, the parents, peace of mind and, often, allow for more patience and grace as you have a more complete picture of your child.*

- *It can give a child a concrete understanding of how they best learn and can help many understand why some academic tasks are a challenge.*

I have not one but two children with dyslexia. Two different types of dyslexia and two completely different learning styles. (Because of course they couldn't possibly have the same diagnosis—some of you know exactly how this feels.) I, clearly, have a background in education and conduct diagnostic testing for other families, but I knew it was important to have unbiased diagnostic testing completed. It gave me peace of mind and another springboard, which allowed me to make a solid educational plan moving forward. Seeking outside testing and assistance is not a sign of inability but a sign of great wisdom as a homeschool parent.

Seeking outside testing and assistance is not a sign of inability but a sign of great wisdom as a homeschool parent.

A Little Encouragement as You Get Going

So, you've decided to try homeschooling your unique learner, but you are worried whether or not it is going to work. Let me be the first to tell you: it absolutely can work. Homeschooling allows you to tailor curriculum, life skills, and experiences to your child's natural abilities, and it allows you to link learning to their interests, which can further propel your child forward academically and help them to find their niche in life. Homeschool allows time and opportunities to take rabbit trails, as we've talked about in an earlier chapter, and those trails can greatly impact a child's confidence and ability as they move toward living life on their own. Following rabbit trails and interests can also build intrinsic motivation and further a child's willingness to complete their schoolwork. You also have the opportunity to use resources and interests to teach cross-curricular. Maybe memorizing facts comes easily for your child, but only if they relate to video games. Luckily there are books on video gaming. Your child can read them. There are math practice books and drills with Minecraft and other video game themes. Your child can practice their facts through these resources. Maybe Pokémon is the only thing your child is interested in. You can use those cards to explore adjectives, adverbs, and writing exercises. This flexibility to tie learning to your child's interests has proven to be extremely helpful with many of my special-needs clients.

Sharing My Personal Experience

When I decided to homeschool I did not know I would be homeschooling two children with dyslexia and one who, quite literally, bounces off walls, but here we are and I am so thankful for this time with them. Instead of my children receiving a few minutes per day of specialized attention in a traditional classroom setting, we are able to consistently address their dyslexia through a specific curriculum. As homeschoolers we have a smorgasbord of curriculum at our fingertips, and they range in intensity. For example, language arts options for mild to moderate dyslexia include Logic of English (one of my personal favorites), All About Spelling, Touch-type Read and Spell, Heggerty, or UFLI (University of Florida Literature Institute). For students with more severe dyslexia, options include Barton (tried and true), Take Flight with a CALT specialist (Certified Academic Language Specialist), and SPELL-Links, among others.

It is important to find the right fit for your child's learning style, but the many options make it possible. For math, RightStart is a wonderful tool for those with dyslexia, as it offers a hands-on component. For children who need to master one particular concept at a time and have ample room on a page to complete problems, along with clean lines and minimal distraction, Math-U-See has proven to be helpful. Teaching Textbooks offers an adaptive and interactive option. Math with Confidence offers a gentle but thorough curriculum for both neurotypical and neurodivergent learners. Math Mammoth has been my family's go-to choice because it includes a variety of learning approaches, visual representations, and a plethora of resources. It is rigorous, but the variety of problems and visuals are extremely helpful (it is great for both neurotypical and neurodivergent learners, as are all of the aforementioned curriculums).

Sometimes finding the right curriculum is game of trial and error, but that is no different than what would occur in a traditional classroom setting. *One program does not fit every child's needs.* Choosing sample lessons and completing placement tests can be extremely effective in narrowing down your options. I honestly wish I had some of these spectacular resources at my fingertips when I was a classroom teacher. How lucky we are as homeschool parents to have a wide array of curriculum! But do remember: there is no magic wand or perfect curriculum. Consistency, time, and patience come into play no matter what curriculum you choose.

It is also more than okay to outsource teaching. Yes, I said it. You can hire a tutor who is trained to work with dyslexia and auditory processing disorders, as well as other learning challenges. There are many certified special education specialists who now offer both in-person and virtual sessions. There are professionals who are extensively trained in Orton-Gillingham who can assist your dyslexic child in making meaningful academic progress. This doesn't mean you are failing at homeschooling. In fact, I would boldly state it is quite the opposite! You are making the best educational choice for your child's learning needs. You also need to protect your relationship with your child, so even if you have completed the training for a program and you and your child are working together but constantly end up frustrated, you may want to seek outside help. This doesn't mean you have failed. It means you are protecting your relationship with your child, and that matters a great deal in the long term. Connection over curriculum, always.

I want to take a moment to mention a couple of curricula, which I have seen produce great fruit for many clients with children who have Down syndrome. Memoria Press offers a special-needs curriculum entitled Simply Classical. I've suggested it to many clients who have reported back positive progress and who felt it was a breath of fresh air. Remedia Publications offers a wide variety of curriculum for special-needs students, including many life skills topics. Able2Learn is a curriculum developed specifically for autistic children. It offers a variety of topics.

Another option is implementing a curriculum with a base in literature, especially if audiobooks resonate with your child. Bookshark and Beautiful Feet are two great options. I would caution you to not try to read every book on their list, but instead pare it down to books your child will enjoy so it can be a fruitful experience. Using any of the curriculums I mentioned earlier in this chapter, but at a grade level that best suits your child, can also lead to a much more meaningful academic experience.

Please know the curriculums I have mentioned in this chapter are those I have used personally or seen fruit with through clients. They are not advertisements, in which I am receiving any sort of kickback. Also know, there are many other options out there. It takes time to research and narrow down.

A Bit of Helpful Advice

If hiring a professional tutor or teacher is too much of a financial burden, there are other options, although they may take a little bit more work on your end. My favorite option: other homeschool moms. Listen, the homeschool community is one of the most intelligent, helpful, and giving communities I have ever been a part of. It is truly astounding some days. If you can find another mom and leverage each other's talents, it is a game changer. Maybe you are excellent at sewing, speaking another language, mathematics, or a musical instrument, and they have the patience and educational background to assist your child in reading. You can swap services or create a small pod that meets on a regular basis. Not comfortable using your home? The local library or community center can be a great place to meet. Relying on other moms can not only assist your child but also strengthen your community, which is so valuable and important when homeschooling.

On a Personal Note

I wanted to share my personal experience, as the entire purpose of this book is to have a candid conversation about homeschooling. I have one child who is so bright, but also so very strong willed. We worked together four days a week using an Orton-Gillingham program and he made great strides, but his personality did not want to make small strides. He wanted leaps, which can be difficult with dyslexia. This led to frustration for us both. My solution? Allow for outside help. Yes, you read that correctly. I am a professionally trained teacher with a master's degree. I am trained in Orton-Gillingham. I evaluate, tutor, and test hundreds of children each year, but I knew I needed to be humble and allow for someone else to assist him for both our sakes. We still did the majority of school together (including our own Orton-Gillingham program), but he also met with a well-qualified, patient, kind tutor who is not his mom. It was a blessing. It built his confidence and it took a bit of the pressure off our relationship. It was the healthiest decision for us both. It was not a failure. It was appropriately supporting his educational needs during this season, while preserving our relationship. Remember: connection over curriculum, always. Our relationship with our children will far outlast the years of homeschooling, so if you continue to hit a brick wall or your relationship with your child is falling apart, it is time to take a step back and reassess.

I teach online and in-person writing classes, and I cannot tell you how many of my students have moms who were (or are) teachers. Teaching your own child, unique needs or not, can be challenging. Do not feel less-than for seeking outside help. One of the perks of homeschooling is being able to pivot and meet the needs of your child to ensure long-term success. Don't put yourself on an island; use your community and the resources available to you whenever the needs arise.

One of the perks of homeschooling is being able to pivot and meet the needs of your child to ensure long-term success

A Brief Word of Caution

I do want to offer a word of caution when hiring tutors: do your due diligence and check references, certifications, and training before investing money. I have, unfortunately, had to tell clients that a tutor they were using took one or two classes in a specialty but were not fully trained, which resulted in frustration and their child's progress stalling, not to mention a loss of time and money. Trained and certified are not the same. It is smart to ask questions before hiring specialists. Here is a list of suggested questions to go over prior to implementing services:

- *What certifications do you currently have that support this area of need?*

- *How long have you been tutoring in this field?*

- *Do you have three references I can call?*

- *What would your plan of action be? How would you pivot if it is not working?*

- *What specific program will you be utilizing?*

- *If you are not using a program, how will you ensure progress and track lessons?*

- *How will you assess my child's initial needs and learning gaps?*

- *How will you monitor and communicate progress?*

- *How can we work together to ensure success?*

- *How do your lessons adapt to fit the needs of different learning styles and personalities?*

- *What is your availability? What happens if you need to cancel or reschedule?*

- *What is your rate and how do you take payment?*

- *What is your policy regarding background checks? *Please background check anyone working with your child, online or in person.*

Tips to Address Some of the Most Common Struggles

Because I do work with many families whose children have special needs, I get many questions on a reoccurring basis. I want to address some of those here.

Problem: My Child Won't Sit Still to Do Work

Okay, I hear you, but first I have a couple questions about your child's habits:

1. *How long can you sit still to do work without going crazy?*

2. *Are you asking them to sit still before or after movement?*

3. *Are they sitting around watching television or playing on screens before school?*

4. *Are you asking them to sit for an extended period of time that is inappropriate for their age, let alone their diagnosis?*

5. *Why do you have to always be at a table?*

Annoyed with me yet? Possibly, but hang in there. Sometimes we need to reflect on what we are asking our children to do and why we are asking them to do it in that particular way. Let's talk about questions one and four first. If most adults were honest with themselves, they would admit that they don't love sitting at a desk or table to focus on work for more than 45 to 60 minutes on average. One common suggestion is for adults to stand for an average of twenty minutes after forty minutes of sitting—note, that recommendation is for adults, not children. There is also data that shows taking movement breaks positively impacts work productivity. So, if this is the case for adults, we know it is even more so for children because they require significantly more movement throughout the day (as discussed in chapter 1).

So, here are the typical attention spans based on age (according to CNLD Neuropsychology)[9]:

- *2 years old: 4–6 minutes*
- *3 years old: 6–8 minutes*
- *4 years old: 8–12 minutes*
- *5–6 years old: 12–18 minutes*
- *7–8 years old: 16–24 minutes*
- *9–10 years old: 20–30 minutes*
- *11–12 years old: 25–35 minutes*
- *13–15 years old: 30–40 minutes*
- *16+ years old: 32–50+ minutes*

If your child is not neurologically typical, the time they can spend on tasks may be shorter (or extensively longer if they can hyper focus). It is important to ask yourself if you are asking your

---

[9] "How Long Should a Child's Attention Span Be?," CNLD Neuropsychology, accessed February 28, 2026, https://www.cnld.org/how-long-should-a-childs-attention-span-be/.

child to sit for too long. That doesn't mean you should never stretch the time or push them further, but if you are facing daily battles over attention span, this is something to adjust.

It is also good to keep a journal. This can be as simple as a calendar where you jot down your routine and note if there was pushback, shutdown, or frustration. You will see trends. On days when your child wakes up and watches an hour of television first, do you struggle to get them on task? Does your child perform better when they jump on a trampoline or go on a brisk walk first? Anecdotal notes will help drive your success. This is reflection, not criticism of your homeschool. Think of it like a new recipe. You liked the recipe, but the result was not exactly what you wanted, so you are tweaking the ingredients to get the desired result. It works the same way for homeschooling. There is no perfect recipe. Different tastes require different ingredients.

Things to Consider

Here are a few more questions to reflect on if you have a child who lacks focus and has a lot of bottled-up energy:

- *Where are you doing school and is movement part of your daily routine?*

- *Does your child need to wiggle?*

- *Can they bounce on a yoga ball?*

- *Can they stand instead of sitting at times?*

- *Can they use a wobble board or even little bike pedals (stationary ones for under the desk)?*

- *Do they need a fidget?*

I have a child who literally works upside down. Like, in a comfy chair, he is writing a paper upside down. His best work happens this way. Why would I fight that? If he isn't hurting himself, others, or my chair and he is being productive, I am completely onboard. As a classroom teacher I would let students work under desks, in a plush seating area, and even a cave (covered desk). Many students diligently sat at their desks, but my classroom was so much more peaceful when I stopped trying to control students' comfort and preferences. The same goes for my home. Yes, being able to sit at the dinner table and at a desk is a skill I want my children to have (and they do), but there are times when it isn't necessary. Want to do math on the trampoline because the movement releases dopamine and helps you to happily stay on task? Go for it, kid! (I would throw up, but you do you!)

Be honest with your expectations and why you are enforcing some of your rules. Don't control little things just to feel in control. It typically does not end well and the expectations of you, the parent, may be the issue. This is hard to hear sometimes, but the problem isn't always the child's behavior; sometimes it is the adult's requirements. When you do need to transition from flexible seating or teach your child to sit longer, you also cannot expect them to make this leap overnight. Just like when they were babies and they were learning to sleep through the night, it happened in increments and time increased gradually. The same concept applies to sitting still at a desk and directing explicit attention to tasks.

Don't control little things just to feel in control

Problem: Transitions with My Child Are So Hard!

This is such a common frustration. I hear you. This can especially be a problem when kids are asked to stop doing something fun and instead switch to doing something that is more challenging. Some of fixing this is, again, trial and error. I know, that feels unhelpful, but it is just the honest truth. Sensory overload is also a real trigger here. Changing the environment, expectations, and tasks can quickly overwhelm many children. Here are a few quick ways to make transitions smoother:

- *Talk about your day before it begins.* This prepares your children for what is to come.

- *Use a visual list or "schedule."* Please note: the word *schedule* is in quotation marks because I want to caution you to not set concrete times unless you know for certain that you can stick to them. A list allows children to anticipate what is next without requiring you to stick to a minute-by-minute schedule, which is typically difficult to do when homeschooling multiple children. Routines and rhythms are better than a perfect schedule.

- *Set timers.* Visual or auditory timers (such as a watch or an in-home device) are helpful for many children. However, some children with higher anxiety find timers to be all-consuming and then they cannot complete their work. Only use a timer if it helps your child succeed.

- *Transition with a game or hands-on activity.* Sometimes a child's brain just needs a moment. Playing a brief game (think three to eight minutes) is a great way to get children thinking about an upcoming task without overwhelming them. Choose an educational game that relates to your next topic.

- *Take snack breaks.* A great way to lessen meltdowns is to ensure snacks and movement are scheduled throughout the day.

- *Limit screens.* We love and hate them. Screentime in between school activities is a common meltdown trigger that I see in many clients. While screens can be so helpful with children who are not neurotypical, the transition off of them can be painful. If possible, save screens for later in the day or keep them to educational purposes during your designated school time.

- *Offer comfort.* Honestly, a quiet voice and presence are sometimes all a child needs when they are having a hard time.

- *Stop rushing.* Unless it is an actual emergency, stop treating transitions as such. This fuels anxiety and sensory overload for many children. If you find yourself rushing on a regular basis, then you, as the adult, need to revamp your schedule and reprioritize.

Problem: My Child Refuses to Work

This is such a challenging place to be in. I've experienced this as a consultant and teacher. I wish there was a one-size-fits-all answer for this particular issue, but there is not. I do have some helpful tips though.

- *Log refusal times and look for correlation.* Do the refusals occur at a particular time of day? Does your child refuse to work on one particular school subject? Is their refusal tied to hunger? Does it occur on a certain day of the week? A review of your notes can help narrow down your approach or prompt you to change something in your schedule.

- *Ensure healthy habits.* Sleep and food can significantly impact a child's willingness and ability to work. Are they consuming enough protein and healthy foods? Are they sleeping enough?

- *Offer choices.* Many times control is the name of the game. Choices make a child feel like they have some autonomy. For instance, when diving into a new math lesson, you can ask your child if they want to use a whiteboard or pencil and paper. You could ask if they want you to explain the lesson or find a short introduction video. The choices do not need to be grand in nature, but they should be enough for a child to feel ownership.

- *Chunk assignments.* Instead of expecting a child to complete a large amount of work all at once, break up their assignment into smaller, manageable chunks. For example, your child has thirty math problems to complete or fifteen pages to read, but they shut down. They refuse to work. There are most likely tears or angry shouts. Your child isn't being "bad." Their brain is overwhelmed by the task, and when their nervous system is dysregulated, the work cannot be completed. Chunking assignments can help with this by taking away some of the pressure. Circle a few math problems to focus on, take turns reading aloud, and break assignments down into smaller parts.

- *Model what you want to see.* Hearing what to do is not enough for most exceptional children; they need to see it. Modeling in writing, math, and even reading aloud is calming and helpful. It allows for children to mimic and helps them to regulate.

- *Provide the right tools.* Sometimes a smooth pen is better than a pencil. Sometimes a whiteboard is less daunting than a piece of paper. (Take pictures if you need to document completed work.) Sometimes manipulatives are easier than paper and pencil tasks. Learning does not only occur in a workbook or with a pencil. Use what works.

When Life Skills Need to Be the Focus

For some students there will come a time when math and language arts progress is no longer feasible. This section is for those families. It is particularly important to know your state's laws in terms of proof of progress for your homeschooler in this situation. I encourage parents to document academic progress through anecdotal notes, testing (when acceptable), letters and notes from doctors and specialists (including occupational therapy, physical therapy, ABA therapy, speech therapy, medical, and private tutoring), and pictures or samples of work and hands-on skills. Documentation protects you and your child. It is a layer of security that I encourage all parents to use, especially those with children who will not fit the typical academic progress most states require.

There are many real life activities that can show educational progress:

- *Reading and following recipes*

- *Playing board games and independent strategy games*

- *Following directions to assemble Legos, furniture, or other items*

- *Listening to audiobooks, podcasts, and videos with follow-up narration or drawing to demonstrate comprehension*

- *Making a grocery list and going shopping*

- *Learning to use a credit card and bank account*

- *Learning to care for another living thing (such as pets and plants)*

- *Tending a garden and growing food*

- *Working on cars*

- *Executing small and large home improvement tasks (from painting to building)*

- *Giving short, multistep directions in games (Simon Says is a simple example)*

- *Filling out job applications and memorizing personal information, such as address, date of birth, phone numbers, emergency contact, and social security number*

- *Practicing reading and ordering from menus (and paying independently)*

- *Budgeting*

Functional reading tasks are life skills that show academic progress, including the following:

- *Reading signs and understanding what they are asking or implying*

- *Reading medication instructions and understanding dosage and administration*

- *Understanding emergency and safety directions and signs (for fires, tornadoes, etc.)*

- *Understanding commonly used symbols on signs*

- *Understanding commonly used print on signs (e.g., STOP, EXIT, EMPLOYEES ONLY)*

- *Locating and identifying signs in a variety of environments*

- *Reading short, multistep directions (games are great for this, as are recipes)*

- *Reading common social and everyday words (hello, goodbye, menu, order) and understanding their meanings*

Documentation through pictures and videos are helpful when showing academic progress. Calendars and logs are also helpful when showing progress. *Above all, please make sure you know the laws for documentation and proof of academic progress in your state.*

You Can Do It

Homeschooling is hard. Homeschooling an exceptional child can be, well, exceptionally harder. You can do it though. You may need outside help, you may need to do school year round (with breaks), and you will need to give yourself (and your child) grace. But you absolutely can do it. I have watched so many clients reduce their child's anxiety, set them up with life skills that allow them to gain employment, and develop a bond that is so deep and special while homeschooling. This does not mean there won't be setbacks and frustrations, but success is possible. Remember to meet your child where they are. Progress is not always about big leaps; it might be small steps forward and sometimes one step backward. Not all progress is linear.

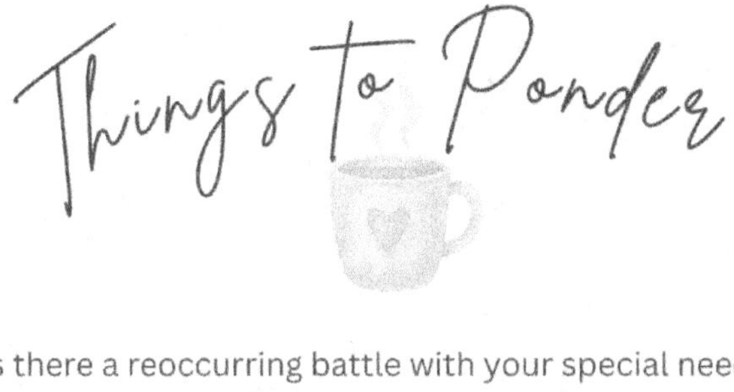

Is there a reoccurring battle with your special needs homeschooler? Can you identify why it is happening? Is it the type of curriculum? Time of day? Your expectations?

____
____
____
____
____
____

Do you feel the relationship with your child becoming strained? If yes, it is time to identify why.

____
____
____
____
____
____

Things to Ponder

What strengths do you see in your special needs child?

____
____
____
____

What progress has your special needs child made recently? Remember, little things deserve to be celebrated. Progress does not always mean a grand leap.

____
____
____
____
____
____
____
____
____

Next Steps

Spend some time celebrating small wins with your child, as a family. These acknowledgements help build confidence in your child, restore relationships, and reframe the focus of your homeschool journey.

Chapter 9

Strategies to Avoid and Overcome Burnout

Burnout can happen to any homeschool parent

Strategies to Avoid and Overcome Burnout

Burnout can happen to any homeschool parent

Homeschooling Is Hard Work and Heart Work

There is no work more important than the work we do inside our homes. I believe this is true, but that work is not always easy, and sometimes we may need a break. I have worked with countless homeschool parents who are on the brink of burning out. My goal in this chapter is to help homeschool moms to recognize the signs of burnout, understand how to prevent it, and know how to overcome it.

Maybe This Is You

"I am not sure if I can homeschool anymore. I am just so tired."
"I think we have to quit. I just can't do it anymore."
"Maybe we made the wrong choice. I am exhausted, and my house is a mess all the time."
"This is just too hard."
"I feel like I am failing."
"I am at my wit's end!"

These are only a few of the many conversation starters I've had with fellow homeschool moms (and dads). Every year I get several emails from clients who are in a panic or are suffering from sheer exhaustion or overwhelm. These are parents who are wondering if they made the right choice to homeschool or why what felt like the right choice at the time feels so dang difficult now. They are exhausted, spread thin, and feel like throwing in the towel. In short, they are burnt out. They just don't realize the signs or reasons behind their feelings.

Signs of Burnout

Do you know how to recognize the signs of homeschool burnout and how to avoid it? I'll let you in on a secret: I didn't for a long time. Truthfully, I am a poster child for burnout. I wish I could say I have never reached the point of burnout, but even as I was writing this book it happened. I tapped out. Not like, I need a week off; more so, do I quit? Am I failing everyone in my life? Can I truly continue working and homeschooling? Obviously, I didn't quit, but you certainly aren't alone if you have thought about it.

Burnout can look and feel like:

- *Being down or depressed*

- *Finding no joy in daily life, especially homeschooling*

- *Going through the motions, but not thoroughly*

- *Mental exhaustion*

- *Sleeplessness and restlessness*

- *An inability to make decisions*

- *Messes that pile up, with no motivation to tackle them*

- *A desire to throw in the towel and let someone else take over*

- *Wanting to quit*

- *Feeling overwhelmed, when you used to feel life was manageable*

- *Feeling that even small tasks are taxing*

- *Lack of patience*

- *Irritability and anger about trivial things*

- *Feeling as though every day is a bad or hard day*

- *Feeling disconnected from your children and spouse*

- *Feeling zapped of physical energy*

- *Experiencing constant brain fog*

- *Feeling as if you can barely make it through remedial homeschool tasks*

- *Struggling to get out of bed in the morning*

- *Raising your voice often*

- *Becoming snappy and snarky around other homeschool moms (or friends)*

This is a short list of the ways homeschool burnout can manifest. Sometimes these are also signs of depression, so do not hesitate to seek professional counseling if needed or desired.

Ways You Might Burnout When Homeschooling

Too Much Socializing

This one seems silly because homeschoolers aren't really supposed to be that social, right? (Just kidding. As we have discussed, that is a huge myth.) Co-ops, playdates, field trips, and classes can be life-giving and fun, but they can also be draining. Many of these experiences require a large social battery. Sometimes you are meeting with people you click with, while other times you might be with individuals or groups who you wouldn't otherwise befriend. (I am just being honest.) It doesn't mean the people are bad or aren't nice, but they aren't the nacho to your cheese or the guac to your chip. (I'm going out for Mexican tonight, so excuse the references.) I would say one of the hardest things about homeschool for me, personally, is how "on" I have to be for so much of the time.

I like to call myself an extroverted-introvert. I love to be social and I love people, but I also need periods of downtime. Sometimes I socialize alongside my kids until I am running on empty, and that makes me feel drained and then grumpy. It is really important to look at your schedule and ensure you aren't overdoing it. There may be seasons when you can handle being extremely social and others where you need more downtime. That is okay. It is also okay to take a break for a week. (Yes, even from co-op classes.) Isn't one of the main perks of homeschooling that we are not held to a preplanned calendar? It is easy to get caught up in the fear of missing out or to let guilt take over and not take the break you may need, but that is a recipe for burnout. So, adjust your schedule as needed when your social battery is dangerously low.

All Work and No Play

I see this often. You bought all the curriculum, signed up for the classes, and you are "doing school" ad nauseam. You are doing a great job of checking all the curriculum boxes. Give yourself a cookie! A gold star! Dare I say, an A+? But you are feeling irritable. You think to yourself, "If we make it to lesson twenty-six, then we can take a break." So you make it to lesson twenty-six, but everyone is dragging themselves there and everyone's attitudes (including yours) stink. Sometimes you just need to take a break.

Clearly you have to adhere to your state's homeschooling laws and statutes, so please do that; however, sometimes you need to take a beat. Maybe it is just for an afternoon or maybe it is for a few days. Maybe you school for six weeks and then take a week off. Perhaps every Friday you play educational games, get out of the house for a field trip, or watch an educational movie, instead of doing typical bookwork. Whatever the case may be, you need to schedule breaks. You also need to be flexible. If your attitude is bad and your heart isn't in it, how do you think school will go with your child? I am going to guess the result will be loads of frustration, possible tears, and maybe a raised voice. Is that better than taking a break? Even as a classroom teacher I would have to read the room sometimes, check myself, and pull a timeout card. It typically reset everyone in the room, myself included, and then we were actually more efficient when we got back to work.

never underestimate the power of a pause and fresh air

A little sidenote: never underestimate the power of a pause and fresh air. I will never forget when I had a very colicky baby. He screamed around the clock for months. It was draining. A wise neighbor and grandmother came over to help me one evening. She said, "Let's reset him." I remember thinking to myself, "Oh, yes, sure. I will just unplug him and plug him back in." Well, she basically did just that. She walked him outside to our deck for approximately three minutes. He came inside happy as a clam. He needed the temperature change, the scenery change, and the fresh air. This little reset trick works for adults and children while homeschooling, too. Grumpy? Everyone pushing back at the table? Go for a walk. Throw rocks in a creek. Rest by a tree or on a park bench. I promise you'll feel better every time.

Overly Rigid Rules

Listen, I am a scheduler and I love a good rhythm, but it is possible to be too rigid at times. Yes, we need and want our children to make academic progress, but maybe your kid is sick of using their workbook. Can they use a whiteboard, draw with chalk, or verbally respond instead? Math facts are becoming burdensome, and if you use those timed tests or flashcards one more time, they might combust from overuse. Can you play a card game? Play basketball or jump on the trampoline while practicing facts? Can you (gasp) use an app to break up the monotony? Sometimes, we need variety.

Think about it this way: do you want someone to give you the same food every morning and then expect you to do the same three chores directly after eating every day? "Okay, Jenna, here is your daily bran muffin. Now you need to write me a paragraph, do three pages of math, and practice twenty spelling words, so we can check off day number 108." Fun times. That would be a capital N.O. for me, and it should not surprise us if our children feel the same way. I am not suggesting that you forgo the daily writing, spelling, or math routine. I am just saying if you feel like you and your children are hitting a wall, then it is time to switch it up. Otherwise, you all will burn out and it won't be pretty.

Decision Fatigue

Boy, do I see this burnout inducer in the late winter and early spring. Homeschool parents are so stressed where I live during this time of year. Our local co-ops begin registration in February (for September of the same calendar year). For the record, I think this is insane. I wish I could push these decisions off at least until April. It may be like this where you live, too. Regardless of the time of year, at some point you will have to make decisions about co-ops and classes for the next school year. That means you also need to decide what curriculum to use next year if you want to correlate learning. Then you will want to see if there is a sale on your desired curriculum. What will you do if your child doesn't love the curriculum that you are still working on for the current year? What if you don't get into your dream co-op or the class you think would be perfect for your high schooler (because you really don't want to dissect a frog at home next year). Furthermore, if your child is in high school, you may be feeling the weight of transcripts, college testing, and heavy, life-altering decisions.

To be fair, every homeschool parent needs to make these decisions at some point, which will require them to spend ample time researching and weighing pros and cons. But I have seen homeschool moms lose hours of sleep over these choices, and I am here to tell you: constant worry (and loss of sleep) will lead to burnout. My recommendation: stop and take a breath. Yes, you may need to apply to a co-op or register for online classes, so do take the time to plan. But please be aware that your life circumstances might change and that perfect co-op maybe wasn't actually the best place for your family after all. Sometimes you need to trust that the right situation will play out and be willing to walk away or make changes to your plan when necessary.

The same goes with curriculum. Yes, you want to be thoughtful when you choose a curriculum, but you also cannot constantly second-guess yourself. If you do, you will be paralyzed with fear and most definitely experience decision fatigue. My recommendation: stop asking every person you see what they are doing next year and what curriculum they are using. Yes, referrals can be helpful, but are you asking because you need something new or are you asking because you are afraid that you are making the wrong choice? There's a difference. It is also good to remember the grass isn't always greener. A new curriculum or co-op may not actually make your life easier.

Remember in chapter 1 when I shared how to create a vision for your homeschool? Go back to your vision during these big decision-making moments. Remind yourself why you are homeschooling and what your vision is. Make choices that are best for your family and that fit your vision, not out of fear of

make choices that are best for your family and that fit your vision, not in fear of missing out missing out or because you believe there might be something else shinier or better. If you find something that is working, keep going with it and you will be less likely to burn out.

My Experience

I'm about to get vulnerable here, yet again. In chapter 2, I shared how I tend to take on too many things, which has led to burnout in more than one season of my life. (My friends and family who are reading this are rolling their eyes and nodding their heads right now. I know, guys! I am working on it.)

One winter, after the holidays in particular, I was feeling stretched beyond thin and majorly burned out. Once again, I found myself doing all the things for all the people. I had begun making plans to have a lighter upcoming school year, but I needed to push myself to the finish line of this school year.

I was feeling snappy—like, super snappy—at my husband, at my kids, and even some of my close friends. (Sorry, y'all.) I was also feeling paralyzed. I saw the stacks in the school room, the piles of laundry, and the checklist that was left undone. It was like I couldn't make a move. I could not complete one more task, let alone do one more thing for someone else or my head may very well pop right off my body. I was spent. I was mentally exhausted. I was physically exhausted, not only because of the tasks I was trying to accomplish, but also because I wasn't sleeping properly. My brain, once again, could not turn off. I became foggy. I became groggy. Sound familiar?

You know what happens when we get in a burned-out state? We often end up becoming either depressed or anxious. For me, it is the latter. I knew I was burned out when I started to worry about things that did not matter and that I could not control. A person who is more likely to get depressed may do the opposite and just stop caring about anything or feel like giving up. Burnout can occur at any time (and I have shared some of my own instances), but there are many situations where burnout is more common than you think.

The first year or two of homeschooling can certainly be difficult. There are many hurdles to overcome: choosing curriculum, understanding how your children learn, learning to manage your time, making friends, and balancing school and life. Despite those challenges, some may find that the first year or two (sometimes three) of homeschooling can be a honeymoon phase, especially if you are teaching little ones. While you need to teach a kindergartener or first grader how to read and to understand basic math skills, you have freedom in your schedule because school does not take all day. Situations vary: you might have a wide variety of activities to keep your child busy inside and outside of the home, you might be juggling babies and toddlers on top of homeschooling, or, quite frankly, you might be bored. So while some may find the first years to be a honeymoon phase, others might find themselves in burnout mode quickly.

As children get older, in third through fifth grades, the demands of education can begin to rise, especially if you are in a highly academic co-op. You might feel the pressure of keeping up with other moms and with the expectations of a particular style of homeschooling. This can lead to fatigue and burnout because homeschooling no longer feels light and free (and full of playdates). Instead it feels heavy and full of unintended expectations.

Then there are the middle and high school years. All of the sudden your child's future seems to weigh on your shoulders. You are faced with heavy questions: Should my child dual enroll at a local college? How do I create a transcript? How will I teach upper-level math when I hated it as a teenager? Plus, hormones and mood swings add another complex layer to homeschooling. Some kids want to fight for more independence at this age, while parents may want to push for their child to take greater ownership in their education. Either battle is tiresome and can make you wonder if you are doing anything right. You may begin to feel like you are constantly chasing your tail because you are worried about signing up your child for the right classes and making sure your child is with their friends, ensuring they get a typical teenage experience. Or maybe you are looking at colleges and trade schools while hoping that you are guiding your child in the right direction. The pressures are seemingly never-ending.

Some lucky families might be in all of the aforementioned stages. Perhaps you have littles who need large amounts of attention and character training to focus on life skills and habits, while you also have teens who need real-life advice and some days need a kick in the rear to finish an assignment. You are grappling with both ends of the spectrum, and you end up feeling like you are treading water. Burnout doesn't only happen to homeschoolers with littles or those whose children are college-bound; it happens to everyone.

I Am Weary. Now What?

Maybe you are feeling burned out right now, and you are thinking the last thing on the agenda is rest. But I am here to tell you: rest is not a form of self-care. Rest is crucial for your mental and physical well-being. Self-care is not taking a shower or addressing your daily needs, nor is it eating cookies in a closet. (Although that might feel like self-care in the moment—I've been there.) Of course, those moments can give you a brief break, but that is not true self-care.

What is self-care, then? Self-care involves finding and doing something that you are passionate about or that gives you life. Maybe it's not something you do every day. It may be something that you do once a year or once a month, but all moms, especially those who homeschool, should have some sort of outlet that rejuvenates them. It takes thoughtful planning and reflection to find an activity that fills your cup. Again, it may not be a daily event, but I do recommend planning an activity to look forward to, one that helps you feel that you are growing or that lifts you up.

self-care involves finding and doing something that you are passionate about or that gives you life

Some Personal Examples

I am an avid horseback rider and have been my whole life. I really enjoy time with animals and being outdoors. It nurses my soul, as it's very quiet. There's no conversation to be had. While I am very much an extroverted-introvert, I also need moments to decompress. During seasons when I couldn't fit in the time to go riding (or we financially couldn't swing it), I took the dog on a walk early in the morning or late at night, when it is quiet and very few people are outside. Many times I did not even listen to music or podcasts. I just walked quietly, reflecting and enjoying nature.

Cooking, baking, and crafting were activities that also rejuvenated me when my kids were little (and I used their naptime as a break). As my children have become older and more independent, I have been able to go to the gym more regularly. (It is a real sanity saver, both the workouts and my friends there.) I also find moments for riding, walking, reading a book for pleasure, or baking. These activities may not happen every day, but I do intentionally schedule them. It may sound silly to schedule downtime and rest, but doing so has helped me to create rhythms of rest and rejuvenation.

Not only will slowing down and resting help you to not burn out, and they also are a great model for your children. Childhood anxiety and depression are at an all-time high. If your children see you take breaks, they will feel they have permission to do the same. What a gift for them: a happier, calmer mom, and a model of how to step off the rollercoaster of life and take a breather. You are showing your children how to live and enjoy the life that you have been given. Being content, enjoying simple activities, spending time in nature, and caring for ourselves are gifts to our children, even as we also use those gifts to fill our own cups.

Mom Guilt

While I expect that there are some dads and grandparents reading this book, I know my main readers are fellow homeschool moms, and I also know that it is extremely common to struggle with mom guilt. I have watched so many friends and clients drown in it. They feel if they take a break or time for themselves, they are being selfish or neglecting their responsibilities. Please hear this: you cannot pour from an empty cup. You cannot prioritize everyone else but never do anything you personally enjoy. If you do, you will become a shell of a person who most likely resents those around you. Taking time for yourself is not selfish. Resting is not selfish. Rest is a human need.

If you asked your children what makes mom happy, how would they respond? Would they be able to answer? Would they have any idea? Would they be able to list anything outside of what you do to care for them? If you are not answering yes to any of the above questions, then you are not showing your children how to live life fully, and you are robbing them (and yourself) of living life to the fullest.

Please understand, I am not saying that every season will be full of rainbows and butterflies. I realize that some readers may be ready to chuck this book out the window because right now you feel like you have zero time for yourself. I get that. I truly do. I went through a period when my husband was traveling frequently while I was caring for a family member, wrangling a precocious toddler, homeschooling two children, teaching a couple of classes, and running a small business. I had zero time for self-care. If I showered and fed myself, it was a good day. Burnout was an understatement. I certainly had no time for myself. Who would clean my house? Who would prep for my classes? Who would make meals and do laundry, let alone teach my children?

In the midst of this busy season, a friend asked me why I had to clean so much and cook each day. Of course, I looked at her like she had two heads. She kindly told me to let some of it go and warned that if I didn't, I might lose myself in the process. She wasn't wrong. I felt like I was checking all the boxes, but I was exhausted. I was not enjoying many of the activities that we were in, and I just was trying to make it through the day. I sat down and really looked at our schedule. I stepped back from perfection and allowed for some margin. I forced myself to make time, just a little, for something I loved each week. I was so much happier. My kids were so much happier. And, ultimately, I was actually more productive when things weren't so buttoned up. I slept better because I stopped letting myself buy into the lie that I was failing if my house wasn't always perfectly put together or if I missed a playdate or activity. It was like a burden had been lifted off my shoulders.

Final Thoughts

Burnout does not have to be inevitable as a homeschool parent. I invite you to learn from my mistakes. Here is a little recap of my best tips to avoid finding yourself in a season of burnout:

- *Frequently revisit your why and your vision for homeschooling.* This will most definitely help to curb the possibility of burnout, and it will reinvigorate and refocus your attitude toward the mundane tasks that can come with homeschooling.

- *Pare down your schedule and create white space on your calendar.* It is okay to say no to activities and people. Even good activities can burn us out if we are overscheduled.

- *Choose to schedule quiet time for yourself.* This is a complete game changer. It may be hard to find time in some seasons, but it is always a great investment. Even five minutes a day or one hour a week to yourself will reset your mood and outlook.

- *Get fresh air.* Even if you are not outdoorsy, fresh air is a reset. Have a cup of coffee on your stoop. Walk around your block or around a local park. Breathe.

- *Discover what fills your cup and schedule it in.* You cannot pour from an empty cup, and you cannot educate your children and love your family well when you are drained.Have a family meeting about what activities fill everyone's cups, then support each other in making time for these activities.

- *Let go of mom guilt.* Living with the "I have to do it all well and by myself" mindset is detrimental to your health. Learn to loosen the reins of some things.

- *Model rest and enjoyment for your children.* It is a life lesson to discover how to rest and enjoy life, and isn't homeschool about living life together and teaching your children how to live fully?

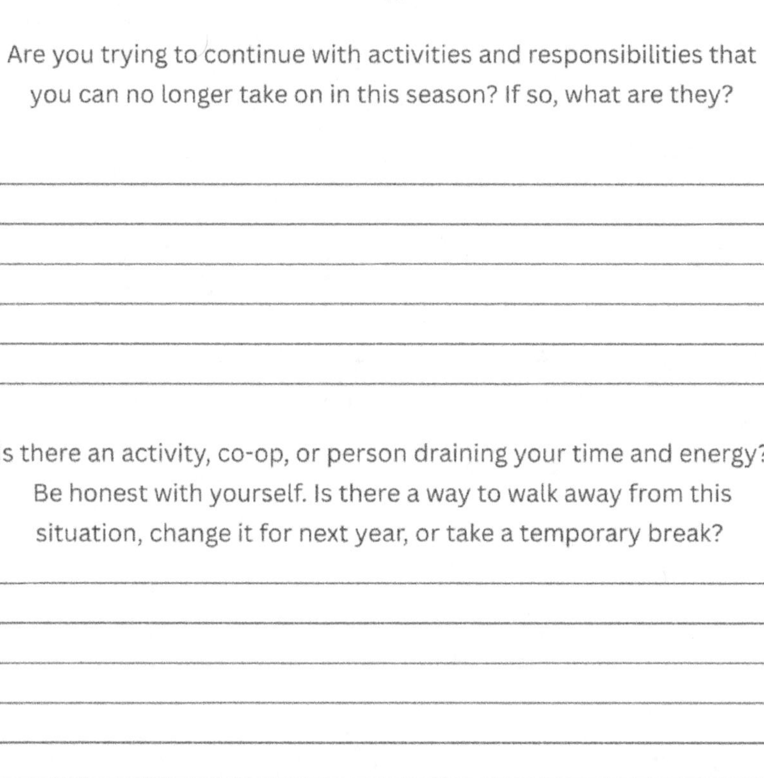

Things to Ponder

Are you trying to continue with activities and responsibilities that you can no longer take on in this season? If so, what are they?

____

____

____

____

____

Is there an activity, co-op, or person draining your time and energy? Be honest with yourself. Is there a way to walk away from this situation, change it for next year, or take a temporary break?

____

____

____

____

____

Are you seeking perfection? Trying to check too many boxes?

____

____

____

____

Are you having fun with your children, or is it all frustration, work, and battles?

____

____

____

Do you have any sort of outlet, quiet time, or hobby that fills your cup? What is bringing you joy?

____

____

____

____

Three steps that I recommend you take this week:

1. Take time to reflect on what is filling your cup and what is draining it. If possible, develop a plan to increase the fillers and let go of the activities that are draining your time and energy.

2. If possible, take a break or schedule something that fills your cup.

3. Revisit your vision and your why.

www.ingramcontent.com/pod-product-compliance
Lightning Source LLC
Chambersburg PA
CBHW071504140726
47997CB00005B/1849